Ghost Hunter's Guide
to
Indianapolis

D1593191

Ghost Hunter's Guide
to
Indianapolis

Lorri Sankowsky and Keri Young

PELICAN PUBLISHING COMPANY
GRETNA 2008

The word "Pelican" and the depiction of a pelican
are trademarks of Pelican Publishing Company, Inc.,
and are registered in the U.S. Patent and Trademark Office.

Library of Congress Cataloging-in-Publication Data

Sankowsky, Lorri.
  Ghost hunter's guide to Indianapolis / Lorri Sankowsky and Keri
Young.
    p. cm.
  Includes index.
    ISBN 978-1-58980-490-6 (pbk. : alk. paper)   1.   Ghosts—
Indiana—Indianapolis. I. Young, Keri. II. Title.
  BF1472.U6S27 2008
  133.109772'52—dc22
                                                  2007047592

Printed in the United States of America
Published by Pelican Publishing Company, Inc.
1000 Burmaster Street, Gretna, Louisiana 70053

This book is dedicated to Danny, my unbelievably wonderful husband. Thanks for listening, thanks for laughing, and thanks for loving me, no matter what. Get up, slug!

Lorri Sankowsky

For Kayden, mon petit amour, and his extraordinary babysitter, without whom my stories would have never been told.

Keri Young

Contents

Acknowledgments

Many wonderful and knowledgeable people assisted in the creation of this book. We would like to thank all those who shared their stories, offered us advice, and allowed us entry into their homes and businesses. Without our friends, family, and trusting strangers, this book would not have come to fruition.

In particular, but in no special order, we would like to thank Mike McDowell and the Indianapolis Chapter of the Indiana Ghost Trackers, Marilene Isaacs, Amy and Chris Garrison, Kim Pratt, Scott Longere, Jarret Marshall, and Mary Ellen Hammack.

Introduction

From long forgotten graveyards and crumbling historic buildings to modern skyscrapers and new housing developments, ghosts are everywhere and they are hot! Interest in the paranormal has skyrocketed, thanks to the Internet and newer technology that allows evidence to finally be captured and scientifically measured. Ghost hunting has gone mainstream, with wide acceptance and a large following. This new interest has spawned books, Web sites, ghost tours, movies, and television programs, all focused on the paranormal. The Travel Channel, Discovery Channel, and Sci Fi channel are airing more paranormal programs than ever before, and the major networks are following suit with shows such as *Ghost Whisperer*, *Supernatural*, and *Medium*.

"The interest in the paranormal is at an all-time high," says Mark Mihalko, editorial director of *Haunted Times Magazine*. "Looking back, it seems like just yesterday we started *Haunted Times Magazine* with a production run of seven hundred issues. That was in October 2005. Now we have an international distributor and a production run in excess of eleven thousand issues and growing."

The city of Indianapolis is known for the Motor Speedway, the 2007 Super Bowl Champion Indianapolis Colts, and as the amateur sports capital of the United States but there is a lot more to the Hoosier State. It has a heritage rich in Native American lore. Native Americans lived along the banks of the White River and Fall Creek and throughout the Indiana Territory. Generations of these spiritual people lived and died, their burial grounds forgotten, blanketed by modern society. Paranormal experts feel that Native American spirits were so powerful that their energy is still present hundreds of years later, resulting in modern-day hauntings.

Interest in the paranormal is alive and well in the Circle City, as described by Nicole Kobrowski, founder of Historic Indiana Ghost Walks and Tours. "We started with tours a couple of times per month, and it has grown from there. Every year we have seen an increase in demand, and now we schedule our tours almost every weekend." Kowbrowski agrees that Indianapolis is emerging as an exciting place to investigate and explore what awaits on the other side. "Many of our customers are coming to Indiana specifically for haunted vacations or getaways. I think for a city that doesn't have the tourism base of Chicago or New Orleans, this has been fantastic!"

FROM INTERESTED BYSTANDERS TO PROFESSIONAL GHOST HUNTERS

We began our trek into the paranormal in 2001, when a combined interest in ghosts led us to a meeting of the Indiana Ghost Trackers (IGT). The IGT is a state-wide non-profit paranormal research group. Mike McDowell, president and CEO, formed the organization. "The Indiana Ghost Trackers started out with about twelve members in August of the year 2000, and it has grown to well over four hundred members. We have maintained this level since 2004, and we currently have twelve chapters all over the state with additional ones planned."

After a few years as members and team leaders, we became codirectors of the Indianapolis Chapter of IGT, furthering our experiences in ghost hunting and investigating. As a result of the hundreds of haunted locations we have investigated, we have witnessed many types of paranormal phenomena. As more and more remarkable things happened to us, we began to discuss the possibility of a book and started researching and investigating on our own, spending many long weekends prowling through haunted buildings and cemeteries.

As we put together this book, we each wrote the chapters that we found the most compelling. Some of the locations we feature were very active, and we were able to gather evidence, but at others, we found little or no activity at all. Ghosts don't perform on command, and sometimes it takes many, many investigations to obtain significant results. In some instances, names in this book have been changed or first names given only to protect confidentiality.

GHOST HUNTING EQUIPMENT

Investigating the paranormal is not an exact science, although equipment does exist that can help prove or disprove ghostly activity. The word "equipment" can mean different things to different people. A scientific person may use the latest gadgets on the market, scoffing at anything that doesn't have dials and laser beams. A spiritual person may prefer a ouija board or a pendulum instead of meters and gauges. We have tried to find an equal balance between the scientific and spiritual extremes and have used a variety of methods in our investigations. We feel that all methods have merits, and you should follow your personal preference.

GHOST PHOTOGRAPHY

There are two things that we never leave the house without, one of which is a digital camera. Entire books on ghost photography exist, and everyone seems to have a strong opinion about it. Major feuds seem to erupt whenever anyone discusses the believability of orbs and/or capturing spirits on film. We have read these various opinions and have decided to draw upon our own experiences as a guideline. There are several well-known and verbose ghost hunters out there who will undoubtedly disagree with us, cite facts and figures, and denounce us as professionals. We can live with that.

What we know is this: Orbs do appear in haunted locations without any explanation, as do mists, shadows, and zigzags of light. Another fact: Neither of us had ever photographed orbs before we began ghost hunting. Piles and piles of family photographs exist, taken with several kinds of cameras, and not one of them has an orb in it prior to 2001. We are comfortable in our belief in orbs as paranormal evidence in spite of the arguments to the contrary. Unless

An orb captured in daylight at Mounds State Park, Anderson, Indiana

otherwise indicated, all photographs in this book were taken by us.

To properly discuss orbs in ghost photography, we should explain what an orb is. An orb is a ball of light, rarely seen by the naked eye but captured on film. Spiritual energy, left behind when the physical body expires, often takes the form least resistant in nature, a sphere or orb. We have used digital media, 35 mm film, and even disposable cameras, and all have successfully photographed orbs. Orbs can vary in size and color; most of them appear as pale gray but sometimes blue, yellow, and even red. They normally appear as three dimensional and have a nucleus, occasionally resembling a human face. Most often they appear at night but not always, as evidenced by Keri's daytime orb captured at Mounds State Park in Anderson, Indiana.

The problem with orbs is that so many things can appear to be a paranormal orb, but really aren't. The main culprit is dust. A lot of haunted locations are old and not frequently disturbed. An inexperienced ghost hunter might enter such an area, oblivious to the dust and dirt that have suddenly been stirred up, and fall over faint when viewing the thousands of so-called orbs that appear in the digital

A green mist photographed on the Gettysburg battlefield in Pennsylvania

camera's viewfinder. Rain can also appear as orbs in photos, as can bugs, sunspots, and lint.

Another anomaly that can be captured with a photograph is called a vortex. A vortex is a swoosh of light, usually white, that inexplicably appears in a photograph. It usually has a curve and is wider at one end, but not always. Most people feel that a vortex is a direct, active passageway that spirits use to travel from this world to the other side. Psychics can often detect a vortex because of the large amount of psychic energy that is present. Catching one on film is a bit trickier; these photos are rarer than orb photos.

One of the most elusive types of photographic evidence is a mist. An unexplained mist taken at an otherwise clear location is very exciting. A mist normally appears white, as if white smoke had floated in front of your camera. Rarely, a mist will be a color. In the photograph above, the mist was an eerie green. This photo was taken at the Devil's Triangle on the Gettysburg battlefield. The white spots are rain.

All photos of mists must be looked at with a critical eye. A mist is one of the easiest things to inadvertently create. Cigarette smoke that is not visible to the naked eye will photograph as a mist, as will fog, exhaled breath during cold weather, and humidity in hot weather. A big cloud of dust from something as common as a dirt road may photograph as an unexplained mist.

The last and most unusual type of ghost photography is an apparition. An apparition is either a face or figure of a ghost. Most of the time, features are fuzzy or nonexistent but the shape is unmistakable. We have been ghost hunting for several years and have never captured an apparition. Not that we haven't tried! It is just that rare to have an apparition make an appearance and even less likely that it would stick around long enough to be photographed.

We mention digital cameras throughout this book many times, however a digital camera is not required to capture orbs. The advantage to using a digital is that the results are instantaneous and you will have a better idea if you are in an active area. A lot of ghost hunters use a digital camera first and then back it up with a 35 mm camera. This allows them to have negatives of their pictures and prevents spending money on developing rolls and rolls of film. We have taken hundreds, if not thousands, of photos that have had no paranormal evidence at all so a digital camera is a wise, but not required, investment.

ELECTRONIC VOICE PHENOMENON

The other item that we always have close at hand is an audio tape recorder. The tape recorder serves two purposes. The first one is mundane; we record ghost stories and interviews so we don't have to take notes. The second reason is much more interesting and involves some of the most mysterious, enigmatic, and sometimes frightening evidence of paranormal activity that we have ever experienced. It is called Electronic Voice Phenomenon, or EVP. It's a long name for what amounts to ghosts on tape. If a spirit has enough energy, it is able to make an imprint on audio tape, resulting in words, moans, sighs, and sometimes complete sentences. Usually this is not heard at the time it is recorded and is not discovered until the tape is played back. EVP can be captured on video cameras, digital recorders, and even answering machines. A dramatized example can be found in the Michael Keaton movie *White*

Noise, where a spirit not only manipulates sound but also the television signal.

We have never had an EVP as dramatic as what is shown in that movie, but we have recorded some very interesting things. Because a spirit is disembodied, it doesn't have a lot of energy. Most of the EVP that we record is barely audible, lots of sighs and whispers, but occasionally we get something fairly startling. We can't stress enough how exciting it is to record a voice from the other side. It is truly the most fascinating evidence we have yet to find.

SCIENTIFIC GHOST-HUNTING TOOLS

Newer and more efficient ghost-hunting equipment is constantly being developed. What we consider cutting edge now will most likely be obsolete in a few years. The equipment that we use is considered standard. Anyone who has watched a paranormal-themed television program knows that much more sophisticated and expensive gadgets are already being implemented; however, we don't have the luxury of an unlimited expense account. The following items are accessible to almost everyone and have been sufficient for our needs over the years. They are certainly not required but do make investigations more scientifically reliable.

An infrared (IR) thermometer. An easy-to-read thermometer that measures temperature fluctuations, instantly substantiating a hot or cold spot.

Electromagnetic field detector or **EMF meter.** A hand-held device that can indicate when there is a fluctuation in the electromagnetic field. It is thought that in the presence of a spirit, the electromagnetic field is disrupted. Escalating readings on the meter indicate the possible presence of a spirit.

TriField natural EM meter. A TriField natural meter detects changes in electric and magnetic energy. If a change in energy is detected, the meter will begin beeping and the needle in the range window will signal the intensity of the energy detected. It is more sensitive than an EMF meter and, therefore, more costly.

Motion detectors. Motion detectors emit a signal when they sense movement in an area, even by unseen entities.

Compass. A compass can detect changes in magnetic energy. This is an inexpensive tool, perfect for a novice ghost hunter.

NONSCIENTIFIC GHOST-HUNTING TOOLS

A sixth sense can be an invaluable tool when ghost hunting. Psychics and sensitives have been able to develop this sense, however everyone possesses some kind of psychic ability. The tools below can be used by anyone who has an open mind and is willing to accept psychic evidence.

Dowsing rods. Dowsing rods have been used for centuries for divining water sources, unmarked graves, and ghosts. Two *L*-shaped rods are held perpendicular to the ground. When they cross or point in one direction, it's an indication of where a spirit or energy might be.

Pendulum. A pendulum is an object, usually a crystal, that is attached to a string or lightweight chain. Its movement can be used to answer questions or point to areas of spiritual energy.

Ouija board. A board and planchette device used to communicate with the spirit world. The user asks questions out loud while lightly touching the planchette. The planchette moves over the board, pointing to letters and eventually spelling out words. Some ghost hunters do not recommend using a ouija board in investigations. Often the spirit who has been contacted is not who or what it appears to be.

Although this book was years of hard work in the making, we have had a lot of fun getting it done. We've met interesting people and experienced unbelievable things along the way. We have presented the ghost stories and folklore to the best of our abilities, however their very nature prevents us from authenticating their veracity. On the other hand, the investigations and experiences directly related by us are nonfictional. We hope your interest is piqued by these pages and you'll want to continue to learn more about the paranormal. Our sincerest wish is that you enjoy reading about ghosts as much as we like hunting for them. Happy hunting!

Ghost Hunter's Guide
to
Indianapolis

CHAPTER 1

Central State Mental Hospital

(Lorri Sankowsky and Keri Young)

"Basement dungeons are dark, humid, and foul, unfit for life of any kind, filled with maniacs who raved and howled like tortured beasts." These are the words superintendent Dr. Everts wrote to the governor of Indiana in 1870 regarding the appalling and wretched conditions of his understaffed and poorly maintained mental institution. His pleas for aid went unheeded, and thus began the twisted and inhumane nightmare of Central State Mental Hospital.

Central State began its existence as a hospital for the insane in 1848. It opened with only one building on a campus of more than one hundred wooded acres on the outskirts of Indianapolis. As the only mental facility in the state until 1905, Central State expanded soon after it opened to include male and female dormitories, an administration building, a chapel, an amusement hall with billiards and bowling, a bakery, a firehouse, and many other buildings the facility would need to house and treat hundreds of patients and workers.

These later buildings were built with an eye towards beauty. The grounds included garden paths, benches, groves of trees, and picnic areas. With its parklike setting, ornate Victorian buildings, train station, gardens, and fountains, a nineteenth-century visitor strolling the grounds might find the rolling hills and trees calming and peaceful, totally unaware of the horror that flailed and strained in the darkness, just beneath his feet.

The treatment of mental illness was in its infancy during the early years of Central State. It was barely understood and hard to diagnose. The term "insane" was freely applied to those who were considered

21

"simple" or "depressed," as well as to those who suffered from schiz-
ophrenia and dementia. This resulted in the mentally retarded being
treated similarly to those who were considered criminally insane.
Doctors were unsure of treatment, and the hospital aids were poorly
trained. Proper drugs and therapy had not yet been invented, and the
only known "treatment" was restraint and punishment.

The worst of the patients, those who screamed relentlessly or were
hostile to the staff or other patients, were confined to the dungeons.
The tiny, dank dungeon rooms were scattered through the five miles
of underground tunnels, which snaked like a labyrinth under the
property. The tunnels were originally intended as a safety measure for
the staff. If a riot or disturbance broke out in one building, they could
dash into the tunnels and get to a safer place quickly. Some of the
Victorian doctors and attendants had another use for them as well.
They believed that the mentally ill could control their actions and
were to blame for their own deviant behavior; therefore, when they
became uncontrollable, they were punished. The worst patients were
chained to the dungeon walls with shackles and left in the darkness,
sometimes for days at a time, with nothing but their own madness.
Although no one would confirm it, it was widely rumored that, when
renovating the tunnels in the 1950s, workers uncovered old shackles
and chains bolted into the tunnel walls.

The punishment did not end there. Patients in the "normal" wards
had their own treatment to deal with. Some slept on beds of straw in
buildings with leaky roofs and moldy walls. Those lucky enough to
sleep in beds were often restrained with leather straps attached to the
steel bedposts. Attendants were known to strike patients, withhold
food, lock them in closets, and restrict them from communicating
with each other. Sometimes window wells were used as outdoor cages,
complete with bars over the top so that patients could be outside but
still confined.

Over time, reform-minded superintendents and community
activists successfully lobbied for more funding, drawing attention to
the patient abuse. Public awareness, as well as strides in treatment,
forced sweeping changes, and conditions began to improve. Social
activities and vocational rehabilitation were introduced. Life at
Central State improved for the majority of those within its walls.

However, the allegations of patient abuse and neglect continued through the years.

These stories combined with a lack of funding, overcrowding, and outdated facilities resulted in Central State's closure in 1994, ending 146 years of service. It was purchased by the city of Indianapolis and now houses a fire department, several offices, softball and soccer fields, and the barn for the Indianapolis Metropolitan Police Department's mounted patrol.

Yet the saga of Central State does not end with its closure, and some even say that the story just begins there. The energy, anguish, and horrors of those who were abused there, as well as those who spent their lives there in the scarlet fog of insane fury, combine to make Central State one of the most haunted areas in Indianapolis. Many people who drive past it on West Washington Street glance fearfully out their car windows at its menacing black iron fence. Children who live in the adjoining neighborhoods give it wide berth during their nightly play. When darkness creeps across its lawn, marking the setting sun, the ghosts of Central State come alive.

Manifestations and unexplained sounds are reported throughout the grounds of the hospital. Reports of ghostly sightings have been received from administrative workers, groundskeepers, and even residents of the adjoining neighborhoods. Mysterious people have been seen wandering the grounds but, when approached, disappear. More than once, calls have been made to 911 to report that patients appeared to be hanging off the fences of the property, arms outstretched and begging for help. These calls came years after the mental facility had been closed.

Security guards have been called when lights have been seen flickering on and off and "people" are moving around in the empty buildings after closing. When they enter the empty dormitories, many guards have reported seeing robed patients running down the hallways, only to disappear into solid walls. Personnel working late in the administration building have seen both ghostly nurses and patients in the hallways.

Moaning sounds, the rattle of chains, and whispers have all been heard coming from the underground tunnels. On the grounds, under a grove of trees, a long-ago patient was stoned to death by another patient. Those who dare to walk past this area at night can still hear his screams. One poor soul who has eternal hopes of escape has been seen repeatedly dashing through the gates and out onto Washington Street. He appears to be wearing a white hospital gown and has been seen by both those inside the property and homeowners who live nearby. The old power house has its share of occurrences, too. A woman's screams have been heard coming from the basement, shadows have been seen darting along the walls, and equipment has turned off and on of its own accord. Especially disturbing is the experience of a worker who fell asleep there and awoke as he was being choked by something unseen. He leapt up and found his neck imprinted with deep red marks.

If tortured, abused patients weren't enough reason for Central State to be populated by ghosts, perhaps the problem is accentuated by the numerous unmarked graves on the property. In July 2003, *The Indianapolis Star* newspaper reported on the graves and how they might affect the usage of the property. Records and fieldwork suggest that the northwest corner where Vermont Street meets Tibbs Avenue is likely the site of a significant cemetery. More human remains were found along the western edge of the property and also around the old pathology building, where hundreds of autopsies were conducted. No one is sure how many unmarked graves may be located on the property. Could those who lay forgotten in the soil, whose remains have been disturbed by stray dogs and gardeners, be responsible for the unrest that surrounds this area?

We first visited the infamous abandoned Central State Mental Hospital in search of possible paranormal activity on a cold November night just after sunset. After studying plans of the buildings, we chose the administration building as our central command center. We unpacked the equipment, coordinated walkie-talkie frequencies, and waited for our guide to unlock the buildings to be investigated.

First stop on our investigation schedule—the dormitories. Numerous paranormal activities had been reported from the dormitories, and we were excited to see what evidence we might be able to turn up. Our guide led us into the drab institutional gray cement-block building and within minutes of stepping onto the first floor, the hairs on the backs of our necks began to stand on end. The first room we entered was a large recreational area with a glassed-in observation room along the back wall. There was no power in the building so it was dark, cold, and completely silent. The recreation room had olive green industrial couches and a scattering of overturned chairs. Eerily, there were still banners and cards reading "Happy Birthday" on the yellowed walls, with long ago deflated balloons scattered around the dusty floor.

We began taking equipment readings and snapping preliminary digital photos. The area felt unusually cold, even for a Midwestern November. Our digital thermometers were picking up several cold spots, one registering an eight-degree drop and the other a remarkable eighteen-degree drop. Severe temperature drops or cold spots can signal the possible presence of a paranormal entity. There was something or things in the room with us.

We tried to be very quiet, hoping to pick up any unusual sounds. From behind the glass observation area came the very faint rustle of paper and then a small bang as something hit the floor. Everyone turned as one, holding their breath, straining their eyes in the dark. We snapped a series of digital photos in that direction. When the photos were displayed on the viewfinder, several large orbs and a sprinkling of smaller orbs were visible inside the glass room and on the walls surrounding the enclosure. The group decided to separate and do in-depth investigating throughout the floor. A few people stayed in the recreation room, and we, along with two others, headed off down the hallway to the small patient rooms that were on both sides of the long hall.

These cells were tiny, just room enough for a single bed, a sink, and a small dresser. Some rooms still had bed frames or dilapidated cheap wooden dressers. As exciting as the thought of seeing an apparition was, the reality of sitting in the dark in an abandoned insane patient's room was really scary. But we did it. We closed the metal door with its small glass window and sat in the dark, dank five-by-five-foot cell. We set up the tape recorder and EMF meter. After turning the tape recorder on, we started asking a series of questions, trying to get a response from any spirit that might be around. Suddenly, the EMF meter made a sharp, quick, shrill beep, which scared the daylights out of us and caused our hearts to race. The meter signals when an electromagnetic force has been detected. A spirit can try to use electromagnetic forces when trying to manifest. What was trying to be seen?

Meanwhile, the other group was getting some fantastic pictures in the recreation room. Orbs and light anomalies were caught in several different locations in the large room. They did some EVP as well and played the tape back after asking their questions. After several minutes of silence, a whispered, drawn out "no" could be heard, followed by more silence and then what sounded like, "We [or maybe you] shouldn't be here". Spooky!

After the initial EMF blare, nothing materialized and nothing moved or made its presence known in any other way. But the room made us uneasy, more from imagining what it must have been like to be locked in this tiny room year after year than from any ghostly activity. We were more than ready to go back to the recreation room with the others. As we were coming into the room, a small movement behind the observation glass caught our eyes, and we both took a quick shot with our digital cameras. It could have been a trick of the shadows, but the blurry outline of a figure, perhaps a nurse, appeared on the LCD screen of one of the cameras! We all concluded the dormitory was a very active place but it was getting late and we had many more buildings to investigate. We reluctantly left that building, vowing to come back when we could spend a whole night there, and moved on to the infamous tunnels.

Our guide led us to a nondescript building where we had to climb down filthy, water-soaked concrete steps to the dirt-floor basement. He unlocked an old rusted door and said, "Here we go! Ready to travel underground through miles of tunnels with no escape if any maniacal ghosts come after us?" He was a funny guy. We turned our flashlights on and proceeded single file, stooping several times to clear the low ceiling. We took initial photos, which produced hundreds and hundreds of orbs. This was a dirt floor in an abandoned tunnel; most of these orbs could be attributed to dust, but seeing a picture of hundreds of orbs blocking the path makes a person pause for a second.

We trekked on and on for what seemed like miles, but in reality we were just going between buildings. One of our investigation team members touched something and asked the guide, "What's this rope that runs horizontally across the tunnel's wall?" Our guide stopped and

Orbs seen in the underground tunnels of the Central State Mental Hospital

grinned at us. He explained that rope was strung all through the miles of tunnels in case of a power failure or riot. If the staff needed a quick getaway route, they could go to the tunnels, follow the rope, and find their way in the dark to a safe place. As we moved down the tunnel, no shackles were found in the walls but those bringing up the rear kept urging us to go faster. When we finally came out of the tunnel and up into the night air near the area of unmarked graves, they said that all through the tunnel they felt something was following right behind them, something that would occasionally blow cold air past their ears.

During its many years of service, Central State lost many of its patients and workers, and a cemetery was needed on the grounds. But sometime in the early 1970s, it was reported that the graves were moved in order to make room for the construction of additional buildings. Those buildings were never built, and it's thought that only the gravestones were removed and the graves still remain in their original location.

As we walked to the far northwest corner of the property, it was clear where the graveyard had been. Even without grave markers, it was obvious this ground had once been used for burials. The ground heaved at regular intervals and subtly dipped, marking row upon row of graves. The undulations were obviously manmade. On the night we were there, moles had been busy tunneling through the soft earth. The grass felt soggy beneath our feet, making the walk difficult. We stopped occasionally to take some digital photographs, careful not to exhale at the wrong moment and record a mist caused by our own breath. Almost every photo contained an orb. Our infrared thermometer showed a steady temperature, no sudden dips or spikes.

In the middle of the cemetery area, we attempted to capture some EVP on a handheld tape recorder, but the noise from the adjacent traffic drowned out any ghostly sounds we may have recorded. As we turned off the recorder and began to make our way to the power house, one of the members of our group found what appeared to be a human bone lying in the dirt beside a small mound, upheaved by whatever animal had been tunneling there. It was ivory colored and small, and although none of us had any medical training, we all agreed it looked like a finger or toe bone. We placed it back in the dirt and covered it again, hoping it was somewhere near where it belonged.

The power house is a large, boxy, brick building once used to supply steam heat to the facility's buildings. Train tracks ran directly behind the building, and cars filled with coal were unloaded onto conveyer belts that would whisk it to the basement where it would be burned to produce steam. Trains stopped running on these tracks when the buildings converted to electric heat, but some night watchmen still tell of hearing the rumble of an approaching train and the sudden sound of a conveyer belt clicking on and whirring to life.

In the power house, we set up motion detectors on three different levels of the building and left meters running in strategic spots. The large building now holds mountains of salt used to melt snow and ice on the property. The salt, coupled with dust, made it hard to breath. After getting the equipment in place, the team sat silently in the dark, waiting to hear any sounds. After twenty minutes, nothing had been heard. We started joking to ourselves that the power house was a bust when the sharp blare of the motion detector went off somewhere below us. Hearts racing, two members of the team went to investigate. They could find nothing that might have set off the detector.

This event remains a mystery. No additional activity was noted in this building, so we decided to move on. After exiting, a member said, "I forgot my compass." He ran back into the building alone. After several minutes he reappeared, pale and shaking. He said, "Did you guys hear a train?" None of us had. He said, "Once I got inside and began walking down the metal stairs to the lower level, I swear the faint sound of a train came from behind those big mountains of salt. It started out very faint but began to get louder and louder. That's when I decided to leave and forget the compass." We stepped back into the building but nothing but silence greeted us.

We moved on to the carpentry building. As we approached, a female investigator with psychic ability remarked that she was beginning to feel apprehensive about entering this building. When questioned, she couldn't quite tell us what she was afraid of; she just knew she did not like this place. But she entered anyway, lagging behind. The first floor consisted of one large room, filled with junk, spider webs, and old parts of machinery scattered here and there. We picked our way through the debris, exploring what the machinery might have been used for, when the sound of wood falling on concrete came from below—one sharp, loud bang. We all stood still, listening. When the sound didn't occur again, we raced each other to the stairs leading to the basement.

Photographs of Central State Mental Hospital's old power house reveal orbs as well.

Once down into the long-unused basement, we took our flash-lights and looked around for the source of the bang. There were so many things lying on the concrete floor we couldn't be sure what had made the sound. We decided to split up and do some investigating of the basement. It was here in the carpentry building that night watch-men had told of hearing dreadful screams throughout the night. One group headed to the west side, and we headed east. Our group had just gotten into place, taking readings and pictures when the sensitive investigator approached us. She said, "I'm not feeling well. I feel dizzy, hot, and like I am going to pass out." Then suddenly, her knees buckled and she turned a sickly shade of white. When she said, "I can't breathe," two guys rushed to grab her and take her upstairs.

At the same time, we began to feel slightly woozy. We often joke that we are the "antisensitives." We wish we were sensitive, but hard as we try, it just doesn't come to us. So, if we were feeling it, there must be something going on. We took photos and readings, and nothing was showing up. With several members of the team getting physical reactions to the building, we were intrigued as to what might be caus-ing it, but further investigation of this building would have to wait until another time. It was well after midnight, and it was time to go.

We have since returned to Central State several times, visiting dif-ferent buildings and experimenting with new equipment. The para-normal activity there never disappoints us. A casual walk along the unmarked cemetery turned up several orb pictures. EVP captured in the old autopsy building, which now houses the Indiana Medical Museum, revealed an unexplained whooping sound from a frustrated spirit. During a nocturnal visit to the old dance hall, a musty, discol-ored crepe-paper streamer floated gracefully, and inexplicably, in the air several minutes before finally plunging to the floor in front of us. Cold spots, sudden unexplainable gusts of wind, and faint whispers are common occurrences.

We continue to receive reports of escaping patients, figures among the trees, and ghostly moans. Whatever the reason, the buildings and grounds of Central State resonate with the sights and sounds of those long past. Nurses and patients continue to walk its hallways, and tor-mented souls taunt those brave enough to descend into its labyrinths, screaming for their final release.

CHAPTER 2

The Slippery Noodle

(Lorri Sankowsky)

Gangsters, the blues, and ladies of the evening. James Whitcomb Riley, John Dillinger, and Billy Joel. The Underground Railroad, moonshine, and murder. Only one place in downtown Indianapolis can claim all that and more: The Slippery Noodle. Built in 1850, it is Indiana's oldest continually operating bar. The building today, at the corner of Madison and East Street, hasn't changed much since its

The Slippery Noodle

birth. The horsehair plaster has been replaced, and the dull poplar wood trim has been exchanged for stunning oak. Neon lights now adorn the gritty brick walls, and the one-time stable accommodates blues bands instead of horses. In spite of the upgrading, the integrity and charm of this fascinating place remains intact.

The Slippery Noodle began as the Tremont House in an era when dirt roads were the norm and the arrival of a train at nearby Union Station triggered great excitement. It was a fine establishment, comparable to the stately and elegant Claypool Hotel, and catered to wealthy railroad passengers. The inn upstairs consisted of several tiny rooms, barely large enough to accommodate a twin bed, a straight-backed chair, and a small washstand. The main bathing facilities were at the end of the hall, and the claw-footed bathtub remains there today. During the Civil War, the inn was a stop on the elusive Underground Railroad, a series of hidden depots used to whisk runaway slaves north to freedom. It was connected to Union Station by a secret tunnel. The fugitives never had to emerge into possible capture, but could silently move from the train station through the dark passageway and into the safety of the inn's basement.

The basement was also used to slaughter the cattle and swine that fed the guests staying at the inn. The gravel floor that soaked up the blood is still in place, as are the meat hooks that hang from the ceiling. During Prohibition, liquor was also furtively produced in the cool darkness. The moonshine still remained in place until the 1970s, when it was finally dismantled.

In the 1860s, the Tremont House was renamed the Concordia House and in later years, the Germania House. It remained the Germania House until World War I, when anything German was to be avoided. It then became Beck's Saloon, which then turned into Moore's Restaurant during Prohibition. After Prohibition, it became Moore's Beer Tavern. It was sometime during this period when the inn ceased and the bordello business was launched. The building changed hands several more times until late 1963, when it was purchased by its current owners, the Yeagy family. After a lengthy debate, they proclaimed it the Slippery Noodle.

The Slippery Noodle has a scintillating history, most of which is based on fact, some on folklore. A few of the older railroad workers who have stopped by over the years claimed that more than a couple murders have taken place within the brick walls, usually executed by gangsters who used the dirt floor in the cellar as a handy disposal site. During Prohibition, the Brady and Dillinger gangs were frequent visitors, using the back building for target practice. The slugs still remain embedded in the lower east wall. There are also bullet holes in the upstairs washroom. The rumor of a grave in the basement has trickled down from owner to owner. Although several areas of the basement have been excavated, nothing has ever been found except the bones of livestock. However, the majority of the basement floor remains undisturbed, perhaps the final resting place for some disrespectful members of the mob.

One documented murder happened in 1953. Two customers in the brothel had a disagreement regarding one of the ladies. Drunk and belligerent, they both stubbornly insisted on the services of the same woman. During the violent argument that ensued, one man thrust a butcher knife into the chest and stomach of his would-be rival. As the unlucky patron writhed on the floor, blood pouring from his lethal wounds, the murderer calmly walked down the stairs and plunked the bloody knife on the bar before strolling out the door. This incident resulted in the permanent closure of the very successful bordello business.

An unproven but entertaining story involves the beloved Indiana poet James Whitcomb Riley, author of "Little Orphant Annie." In his later years, Riley took up residence in an upscale section of Indianapolis called Lockerbie. He was a heavy drinker and a frequent visitor to most of the bars in Indianapolis. He spent numerous nights in the comforting warmth of the Slippery Noodle. When he had imbibed a little too much whiskey, he would step outside and stumble into the pumpkin patch that grew on the north side of the building. As the moonlight reflected off the plump pumpkins, Riley would settle himself among them and converse with them as if they were old friends. He bestowed names to his favorite ones and often stayed into the wee hours of the morning. It is said that it was during one of these midnight visits that he was inspired to write the poem "When the Frost is on the Punkin."

The Slippery Noodle has more than a rich history—it has ghosts.

These are not shy, bashful ghosts who lightly tap on a wall and fade away. The ghosts who haunt "the Slip" like to make themselves known, and they demand attention, boldly stomping through hallways and appearing to those who least expect it.

Owner Hal Yeagy first began his acquaintance with them in the early 1980s. "Downtown Indianapolis didn't have much going on back then," he says. "Sometimes we only had one or two customers in the evening. On those nights, I would lock up the place. I was the only one with keys. I would lock a door with a padlock and then put a two by four across it. Lots of times, I would come back and the two by four had been moved and the padlock unlocked. I knew I had the only key. This happened a lot, doors opening and closing."

Yeagy has never seen a ghost in the years he has owned the bar, but things have happened that he can't explain. There are also certain areas of the building that he refuses to enter. One of them is a mysterious cubbyhole room in the basement, a tiny dirt-floor room with no logical purpose. "I can't explain it but I just stay away from it. I just don't like being near it," he says. The other area that he avoids is the washroom upstairs. He has to go in this room to do some maintenance routines but he doesn't like it and exits as quickly as he can.

Marty Bacon, the personable manager of the Slippery Noodle, has had several unsettling occurrences happen to him, usually after the bar has closed and the customers have left. "Everything seems to happen to me in the back bar area. A couple of times I have been there alone and the cash register drawer has popped out. And they just don't do that. And I've had the television back there suddenly come on, even though it's up on the wall and no one can touch it."

When the bar is empty, Bacon has heard his name whispered and sometimes yelled in an authoritative voice. Several waitresses have also reported hearing their names called out by an unseen customer. At least every two weeks, Bacon hears heavy footsteps going up and down the main hallway. When he is near the stage area, he hears them stomping in the upstairs hallway. He also feels as if he's being watched or, more specifically, supervised. According to a psychic who once visited the Noodle, the ghost who watches Bacon considers him its employee. The ghost boss would express its anger when it felt Bacon was ignoring its wishes.

Bartender Trey Roberts also has a terrifying story regarding the footsteps upstairs. "I was closing up the back of the building, and I was behind the bar, cleaning up. All the lights were off, and there was no one there but me. I had just come from upstairs, locking all the doors, so I knew no one was up there either. Suddenly, I got chilled and all the hair on my arms stood up. I was directly underneath the balcony, and I heard someone walking around up there! It was definitely the sound of boots on the wooden floor, and no one wears boots but Marty, and I knew he was up front. I tried to ignore it, but the footsteps started getting louder, and whatever it was began walking quicker. Finally I threw down my stuff and ran toward the front of the building. When I did, the footsteps sped up, too, and were heading right toward the stairs that led down to where I was, almost running. Man, I was scared! I slammed the door shut and locked it and told everyone I was never going back there alone again."

Feeling that the footsteps were ominous and menacing, Roberts doesn't like to think of what could have happened if he hadn't fled. "When they sped up, there was a reason, and I don't wanna know what that reason was!"

Marty Bacon also says that, while he doesn't feel threatened, he does feel as if someone is trying to get his attention, and there are times when these feelings are more intense than others. "Sometimes it's like someone is saying 'Pay attention to me, dammit!'"

One of the ghosts that appear regularly is described as a large black man in denim overalls. He only haunts the basement and has been seen by several employees. The most recent sighting was by a deliveryman who was taking beer into the basement. As he maneuvered through a narrow passageway, he saw the man standing in the middle of the hall, looking at him. He calmly went upstairs and inquired about the stranger. When told there was no one down there but him, he promptly left and vowed never to deliver there again. A woman delivering paper products has also seen the ghost. She nodded to him as she walked by, and he nodded in return. Imagine her surprise when told she had greeted a ghost!

Another mysterious specter is a woman in a long, turn-of-the-twentieth-century blue dress. She is only seen upstairs and occasionally makes an appearance on the balcony that overlooks the stage.

One evening, a group of waitresses took a ouija board into the tiny basement room, and the planchette spelled out the name "Sara." She has been referred to by that name ever since. No one knows if Sara was a working girl or a traveler, but those who have glimpsed her describe a great sadness in her face. She is frequently seen during closing time by bar patrons who helpfully tell employees to "make sure and get that woman upstairs before you lock up."

Keri and I began our investigation of the Slippery Noodle in the wee hours of a frosty morning in February. The streets of downtown Indianapolis were deserted, and a snowstorm had developed, coating everything with a veil of white. The bar had closed at midnight on Sunday. We arrived about an hour later, accompanied by several members of the Indiana Ghost Trackers. A band was packing up its instruments and hauling out equipment, and the stage still reverberated with energy. All the nonessential electricity was turned off so it wouldn't affect any of our meter readings.

We began our investigation in the basement, which is not one big area but is divided up into several narrow passageways and rooms. Some of the rooms are used for storage, while others remain empty. Sections of the floor have been finished with concrete but other sections are still only gravel. The gravel crunched under our feet, sending small particles of dust into the air and rendering our digital cameras useless. The temperature dipped as we walked deeper into the caverns of the basement, following the winding passageway. There was a strange but not unpleasant smell of age and asphalt.

We ended up deep inside the basement in an inky-black storage room filled with extra chairs and other furniture. Through the upright chair legs, the outline of the tunnel that once led to Union Station could still be seen, illuminated only by our flashlights. It was bricked up several years ago but it is easy to imagine road-weary slaves, stumbling through the darkness with lanterns. We took a few test pictures with the digital camera and only got more dust orbs. As we stood, reviewing our pictures, the area got noticeably colder. The infrared thermometer never wavered, but the extreme temperature drop was physically felt by all.

I queued up my tape recorder to attempt some EVP. We stood motionless and silent, watching our breath as we exhaled. I asked the first question, a provocative one that always gives me a little thrill. "Is anyone here?" I paused, waiting for a response that would only be heard when we played back the audiotape. As I started to ask the next question, Keri nudged me and pointed above us to a maze of utility pipes. Inexplicably, a black plastic rosary had been looped across one of the pipes, the cross hanging down. It slowly started swinging back and forth. I asked another question. "What is your name?" The cross swung faster.

"It could just be a draft" Keri said, as we stood watching. After she spoke, the cross arced and, instead of going backwards and forwards as expected, it began to swing in a circular pattern, eventually changing from swinging back and forth to left and right. Astonished, we resumed recording EVP. The air warmed, and the movement of the cross slowed and eventually stopped. We checked to make sure the heating and cooling system had not been accidentally turned on. It had not been touched, and the IR thermometer had not noted any temperature change.

Our next stop during the investigation was the balcony where Sara, the "blue lady" had been seen. The balcony is in the back area of the bar in what used to be the stable and now overlooks the stage. As soon as we climbed up the steps, our EMF meters began flashing and trilling, indicating the presence of electromagnetic energy. We slowly walked the area and noticed the EMF meter was especially lively when held over a small round table. We couldn't find any electrical wires or discern any other source that might have caused such a reaction.

We decided to use the compass. A compass can work as a rudimentary magnetic meter. It is a low-cost alternative to an EMF meter and can be purchased in any sporting-goods store. The compass was placed in the middle of the table and illuminated by a flashlight. I began to speak to Sara, explaining to her that we believed she was there, and asked her to prove her existence. The needle on the compass began to tremble. Trying to prevent any vibration that might affect the compass, we made an effort to stand completely still. The needle continued to flutter then, slowly and deliberately, it turned in a clockwise motion. Looking at each other in amazement, we redundantly asked, "Sara, is that you?" I'm sure poor Sara was getting exasperated with us. As if to prove her point, the flashlight in my hand began to dim. As we watched in absolute silence, the beam got weaker and weaker and finally went completely dark.

I banged the flashlight against the palm of my hand, and it sprang back to life. We quickly packed up our equipment and departed the balcony, leaving Sara at peace. The EMF meters continued to register consistent spikes around the main stage, probably picking up the electrical wiring. Keri did obtain a curious digital photo of a streak of orange light that seemed to be shooting across the room.

The owner, managers, employees, and even customers still experience unexplainable occurrences almost daily. Wine bottles are found uncorked, doors open and close on their own, and the ever-present footsteps still trod up and down the hallways. I highly recommend visiting the Slippery Noodle for its scrumptious food, fun atmosphere, and live blues bands. If you're lucky, you might have your own encounter with one of its resident ghosts.

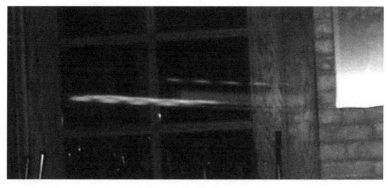

A curious streak of orange light appeared in a digital photograph taken at the Slippery Noodle.

CHAPTER 3

Haunted Theaters

(Keri Young)

Ghosts love drama. Or so it seems. With so many theaters in town boasting a specter or two, it would seem some ghosts just want to be stars. Indianapolis is home to more than twenty different theaters, and several have a resident ghost or two. So sit back, relax, and enjoy the show—if you dare!

INDIANA REPERTORY THEATRE

140 W. Washington Street
Indianapolis

The Indiana Repertory Theatre (IRT), located in the heart of downtown Indianapolis, is the Midwest's premier, not-for-profit regional theater. Each year, Broadway productions, musicals, and award-winning local plays are featured on its three stages. The IRT is housed in what was once the Indiana Theater, a grand movie palace built in 1927. The Spanish baroque-style theater had terra-cotta and marble façades, travertine-marble floors, and a Rookwood tile fountain. Originally, the Indiana Theater building contained a 3,200-seat auditorium, diner, soda fountain, candy store, and basement bowling alley.

On the top floor is the famous Indiana Roof Ballroom, which in the 1930s and '40s was *the* place to see and be seen while toe tapping to the era's top big bands. It was state of the art for its time and resembled the courtyard of a Spanish coastal village, complete with a nighttime sky adorned with twinkling stars, clouds, and a crescent moon. It even had a sea-salt system that pumped sea air over the

Indiana Repertory Theatre

audience. Today The Roof is still one of the city's premier spots for formal events.

The Indiana Theater building is not only unique and beautiful, but it's also full of ghosts, one of whom is a fitness buff. The first artistic director of the IRT was an avid runner who never let bad weather stop him from getting his daily run. If it was rainy or cold, the resourceful director would use the upper mezzanine area of the theater as his indoor track. He did this for years until one rainy, foggy night he went out for a quick jog around his neighborhood and never returned. His nephew accidentally struck and killed him with his car in the thick fog. Ever since that fateful night, when it rains, the creaking of floorboards can be heard coming from the mezzanine area, in rhythm to a runner's stride. A costume assistant said one late night she was working alone in that part of the building when she heard creaking coming from above her. Because she had heard the story of the running director, she quickly gathered her costumes and equipment and finished her work at home.

Another ghost is said to be that of a homeless man who was trying to find a place to sleep one night between the IRT building and the

Embassy Suites Hotel next door. He accidentally fell from the street level of Washington Street, somehow landing on the concrete of the IRT basement floor below. It was several days before an IRT maintenance worker entered that part of the building and found the man dead. But the fall did not kill him right away. On the metal housing of one of the buildings' big heating and cooling units, there were deep scratches and a piece of broken concrete near the man's bloody fingers. He had apparently been banging and scratching on the metal trying to get someone's attention for days before he finally died from his injuries.

Today, it seems he is still trying to get attention. Many on the staff refuse to go into that part of the basement. Maintenance workers have told of strange things going on in the area. Doors have opened and slammed shut on their own, lights have gone out, and scratching and loud banging sounds have been heard when no one is around.

We were invited to the IRT to do an impromptu investigation of the large theater on a night when the houselights were dark and no productions were running. We entered through the ornate glass front doors into the gilded lobby, where the public-relations manager was waiting for us. Lorri and I were accompanied by four other paranormal investigators.

We began our investigation in the main auditorium, where we took test readings on the EMF meter and snapped digital photos. As the investigators went up and down the auditorium aisles, an EMF meter started beeping near the stage. The PR manager said that there were power lines running all over the room. It could have been the power lines setting off the meter, but to be sure we snapped photos of the area. Several large orbs were spotted in the photos.

Amy Garrison, one of the paranormal investigators with us that night, did EVP recordings in the hallway outside the IRT administrative offices. She asked a few questions and then let the recorder run, taking note that there were children playing in a room next door but not making noise that could be heard in the hallway. When she played the tape later, there is a small child's voice saying, "Help me. Let me go." Amy said the children in the next room never said those words. Ghost children are sometimes intrigued by live children. Maybe a little lost ghost child was looking for a playmate.

In the fourth-floor lobby, the group prepared for another EVP recording session. We started with baseline statements, giving the date, time, and who would be leading the questioning. While we were going through the usual questions, I noticed that one of the twenty large glass chandeliers above us was swinging slightly. It swayed gently, almost imperceptibly. When I called out to the others to look, it picked up speed and began rocking slightly from side to side. Lorri exclaimed, "Look, more are swinging." All around the room, chandeliers were slightly swinging. There was no pattern to the movement; one would stop and another would start up, but no group of chandeliers would sway at the same time.

We split up and went around the room looking for air vents and checking for air flow, trying to find a logical explanation for the swaying lights. We found that the air conditioning was not running, and we did not feel any gusts of air. We couldn't be completely sure that this was paranormal phenomena because we were not able to turn off all the electrical systems, but because we did not feel any drafts and there was no uniformity to the movement, we concluded this was pretty good evidence of ghostly activity.

Our next stop was the infamous basement. In the area where the homeless man had lost his life, the group did an EVP session and took digital photos and infrared thermometer readings. In a spot very close to the area near the heating and cooling system, there was a distinct fifteen-degree drop in temperature recorded with the IR thermometer, and the cooling system was not running at the time. Orbs were captured in several areas of the basement and hallway.

Before we ended the investigation, we took a few moments to go backstage in the upstairs theater. The stage was littered with props, and we had to pick our way around scene pieces. But once we had all gotten to the other side of the stage and began an EVP session, one of the large, heavy set pieces on the other side of the room fell down. Was someone trying to get our attention?

THE MURAT CENTRE

502 N. New Jersey Street
Indianapolis

The Shriners are a fraternal organization stressing community service and social interests that developed from the much more secretive and ritualistic society of the Freemasons. The Murat Mosque, in downtown Indianapolis, was the seventeenth temple built for the growing Indianapolis chapter of the Shriners. Erected at the intersections of New Jersey Street, Michigan Street, and Massachusetts Avenue, the mosque would become the largest of the 191 Shrine Temples built organization wide.

In 1909, the mosque was expanded to include the Murat Theater and renamed the Murat Temple. The temple was once again expanded in 1923 to include the fourteen-thousand-square-foot Egyptian Room, social hall, and banquet rooms, and in 1969 a modern addition was added to include meeting rooms and a public restaurant, The Shrine Club. Based on mystic and mysterious traditions, it's no wonder that a Shrine temple would be a welcoming spot for ghosts.

At the Murat Centre, which is the name for the entire complex, actors aren't the only thing capturing audiences' attention at the 3,200-seat Murat Theater. Mysterious blue lights have been seen soaring above the stage, hovering and then slowly dissipating. Always originating out of the same box seat, this phenomenon is seen so frequently that at the start of every new production, the actors are warned to go on with the show and not be alarmed when the light show starts out in the audience.

The box seat where the lights originate once belonged to Elias J. Jacoby, potentate of the Indianapolis Shriners from 1907 to 1912. Jacoby spent countless hours in the temple during his tenure as potentate and through subsequent years as a member. He knew every nook and cranny and often called the temple his second home. He died December 31, 1935, while getting ready for the annual New Year's Eve party at the temple, and some say, he never left.

Shriners and the staff of Live Nation, the production company that manages the Centre, fondly attribute the unusual happenings in the building to Jacoby's ghost. Aside from the blue lights, there are also footsteps in empty hallways, lights that turn off and on, locked doors that swing open and closed, strange knockings, clattering that comes from nowhere, and music that emanates from empty rooms.

A maintenance worker working late one night installing new seats in the theater looked up to the balcony to see a dark silhouette rocking in what he later found out was Jacoby's favorite chair. He could not be convinced to finish the job that night, and another worker was brought in. He, too, saw the specter, and the rest of the seats had to be installed during the daylight hours of the next day. A staff member remarked, "We all think it was Jacoby watching over the renovation to make sure everything was done right." Jacoby's activity seems to escalate during times of change at the temple. He is never menacing, but just seems to be watching out for the building he loved.

Like other former potentates, Jacoby is featured in a large oil painting that hangs outside the Shrine Club restaurant. Unlike the other portraits, this potentate's eyes follow you around the room and on several occasions have actually cried. Lloyd B. Walton, former public-relations director for the temple, wrote of an incident where the portrait seemed to come to life. He had invited ten noted psychics to spend the night in the building, and around 2:00 A.M. they gathered around Jacoby's portrait to do a meditation session. Walton then said that as he was watching the portrait, Jacoby's face began changing expressions. It went from its normal scowl to a smile and miraculously age progressed from a young man to middle age and then to an old withered man. Almost half of those gathered saw a single tear roll down the cheek of the portrait. Two months after that session, it was announced that the theater and the Egyptian Room were to be leased to the production company and to undergo a $12 million dollar renovation.

Jacoby may not be the only ghost hanging around. In 1910, according to the *Indianapolis News,* Edward Cunningham was a twenty-four-year-old iron worker working on the new Murat Theater addition to the temple. He was standing on a high beam when he lost his footing and fell 125 feet. He died from a broken neck before medical help could arrive. Through the years, stage hands have reported a hazy black *X* shape that quickly falls from the top of the theater to the floor of the orchestra pit. This phenomenon has been seen during productions, when the audience is oblivious to it, and when the theater is dark with no one around. Could this be the iron worker with outstretched arms and legs making the mysterious black *X?*

Lorri and I had arranged for an after-hours tour of the Murat Centre complex and met up with our Live Nation tour guide in the ornate lobby of the temple. She told us that the lobby was once a social room for the Shriners. We tried some EVP in this room and tested the meters, but nothing registered. We didn't get any weird vibes in this room, so we moved up the intricately carved staircase to the theater. All the lights were off, and our tour guide left us while she hunted for the mechanism that turned on the stage lights. Standing in the balcony with total darkness around us, we moved toward the famous box seat of Elias J. Jacoby. An ice-cold chill wrapped around me as I touched the seat. We didn't have our IR thermometer for an official reading, but the temperature was markedly colder than when we had entered the theater.

When the lights came on and our tour guide returned, we asked her if she had ever experienced anything in the balcony. She said she had never seen Jacoby but always felt a little scared when she walked by herself down the left-hand hallway that led out of the balcony. We walked out that way. No apparition of Jacoby was seen but it did feel a little eerie.

Near the front row by the stage, I turned around and snapped a picture up toward the center balcony and Jacoby's chair. Later, when I downloaded that photo, there was a large orb directly over Jacoby's seat and smaller orbs on the main floor, stage left.

We moved on to the impressive Egyptian Room, used mostly for big-name musical performances. Our Live Nation tour guide told us that Jacoby's daughter, Helen, had decorated the room with motifs she had found in paintings in ancient palaces and tombs of Egypt. She had also included in the room the likeness of a little-known Egyptian pharaoh named King Tut. Just one year later, King Tut's tomb would be found and his name would become known world-wide. Did Jacoby's daughter know something the rest of the world didn't?

The Egyptian Room has had many reported strange occurrences. Lights turn on and off, music is heard coming from the theater after the building is empty, and security guards have told of hearing the sounds of a great party going on inside the locked doors. Knowing no one was supposed to be there; the guards banged on the door and demanded to be let in. When no one let them in, they got the key and unlocked the doors. Instead of partygoers and a band, they found a dark empty room. We did an EVP session, and upon playback there is whispering on the tape but we couldn't make out the words. There is also a loud knock that we did not hear when we were in the room.

The Murat building is filled with secret stairways, elusive small

An orb is visible in a digital photograph taken of the box seat of Elias J. Jacoby, former potentate of the Indianapolis Shriners. Jacoby's spirit is said to haunt the Murat Centre.

rooms, back passages, and some areas that are off limits to all but members of the Shrine. We could never cover it all with one investigation. On our next investigation, we hope to take digital photos and EVP around the infamous painting of Jacoby and explore more recesses and rooms of the Murat.

THE RIVOLI THEATER

3155 E. Tenth Street
Indianapolis

A little bit of Hollywood history resides right here on the east side of Indianapolis. In 1927, the president of Universal Pictures, Carl

Laemmle Jr., wanted a first-class movie palace built in Indianapolis to showcase his pictures. He commissioned and helped design a Spanish Mission-style theater that would seat more than 1,500 patrons. He instructed the designers to spare no expense, and the finest materials and furnishings were brought in to complete the job. Leaded-glass windows and brass door fittings accentuated the marble floors. In the main theater, there was a central muraled dome over the audience with twinkling lights to simulate the night sky.

During its heyday, the theater hosted Hollywood films and musical performances and thrived in the eastside neighborhood for ten years. The Depression slowly curtailed its audiences, and the advent of talking pictures was particularly hard on the grand movie palaces. In the 1930s, movies with sound became popular and theaters had to install expensive sound systems. For the Rivoli, its grand size made the cost of installing sound equipment too expensive for Universal Pictures. It sold the theater in 1937 to another company that installed the sound system, but the theater never regained its place as a movie palace. Through the years, the Rivoli tried everything to try to stay alive, but it barely scraped along.

In the 1970s, the theater hosted musical acts such as John Mellencamp and Linda Ronstadt but was already getting shabby and run down. In 1976, the theater was bought by another owner who tried to restore it but time and the elements seemed to always be one step ahead of him. The theater doors were closed for good in 1992.

Today the Rivoli is shuttered and the doors are locked. No one goes inside. The once magnificent building is crumbling in upon itself. Ceiling tiles in the auditorium are falling in chunks on the formerly luxurious seats. Water damage has turned the carpeting to mold and dust lays three inches thick on everything. Broken wall sconces, shattered tile, and rotting wood trim litter the floor. The building, inside and out, has a sad forlorn look.

There have been ghost stories about the Rivoli as far back as neighborhood folks can remember. When I asked a longtime area resident what she had heard about the Rivoli, she said, "I used to go see movies at the Rivoli on Saturday afternoons. I would sit up front, and sometimes I and maybe a few others would be the only ones there. I was always turning around because it felt like someone in the back was watching me. But there was never anyone there."

There are numerous stories from former patrons about feeling watched in the theater when no one is there, lights going on and off, movies that would skip without cause, problems with the sound system, and things appearing and disappearing. One moviegoer said that while the movie was going on, a large dark shadow crossed the screen and he didn't see anyone around who could have done it.

The most frequent sighting at the theater is that of a ghostly couple. Theatergoers have told of a weird silent couple sitting near the front. He was dressed in a tuxedo and top hat and she in a long white gown. They never spoke but just stared blankly at the screen, even when nothing was playing. They disappeared if approached or sometime before the movie ended. They have never been identified but have been captured on camera.

A female spirit also roams the halls of the Rivoli. She is seen so frequently and is so benevolent to the theater and those who take care of it that she is called Lady Rivoli. She is described as wearing a long period dress with upswept hair. She has had encounters with visitors in the ladies room, the auditorium, and on the stairs leading to the projection booth. Lady Rivoli is still seen frequently today.

The Rivoli was designated a National Historic Landmark in 2004, and there were plans for its renovation. But as of the writing of this book, no renovations have started. Without help soon, it looks like the Rivoli has a bleak future.

HEDBACK COMMUNITY THEATRE
FOOTLITE MUSICALS

1847 N. Alabama Street
Indianapolis

Footlite Musicals is an all-volunteer nonprofit musical theater in downtown Indianapolis. Started in 1955 as a spin-off from the Catholic Theater Guild, the group performed in high-school auditoriums and theaters throughout the city until in 1974, when it found a permanent home in the former 1924 Civic Theatre building, which the troupe renamed the Hedback Community Theatre.

Even though the Hedback Theatre is an old structure, the ghosts that appear in the building are thought to manifest from the land the theater stands on and not from the structure itself. Before the staff knew the history of the land, they were perplexed as to why Civil War soldiers were seen walking around the basement. After some research, there is a good explanation for this unusual haunting.

In 1859, the state of Indiana took possession of a large parcel of land north of the city, including the land where the present theater resides. The city used these acres for the first State Fairgrounds. The fairgrounds had to be cleared in 1861, when the Indiana state government needed an area to train troops for the escalating Civil War. Camp Morton was hastily created, incorporating the barns and other buildings already on site for the fairgrounds. Here, Indiana troops were drilled and trained for battle.

In 1862, Camp Morton was turned in to a prison camp for captured Confederate soldiers. Of the initial 3,700 Confederate prisoners brought to Indiana, many were already seriously ill from harsh treatment in other facilities. Many were also under the age of eighteen. At the camp, the prisoners received medical attention and nursing care, but some were too far gone to be saved. Camp Morton continued to take new prisoners until the end of the war, when the remaining prisoners were freed.

There are two sides of the story about the conditions in Camp Morton. One version is that the prisoners were treated as fairly and humanely as could be accommodated during war times with scarce funds and that the staff and especially the camp commandant, Colonel Richard Owen, were professional and kind.

The other version is that Camp Morton was a place of neglect and inhumane treatment. Prisoners were routinely starved and forced to kill rats and cats for food and to buy highly valued dog meat on the underground camp circuit to stave off starvation. In the essay "Horrors of Camp Morton," by Dr. John A. Wyeth and published in *Century Magazine* in April 1891, there are allegations of abuse by prison guards and the outright murder of some prisoners for minor infractions. The essay goes on to say that in the winter of 1865, the temperatures in Indianapolis dropped to several degrees below zero for weeks at a time. According to the essay, the prisoners had only thin, ragged clothing and worn shoes and were forced to run in circles all day in the harsh winter climate as punishment. Many prisoners died of the brutal conditions, of starvation, or of outright abuse and murder.

No matter which version is correct, Camp Morton was a place of misery, sorrow, and death. More than 1,600 confederate soldiers died while at Camp Morton and were interred in Greenlawn and City cemeteries.

After the war ended and the remaining soldiers freed, Camp Morton was disassembled, and the State Fair once again returned to the area until 1890, when it moved to its present-day location on Thirty-Eighth Street. The land where Camp Morton once stood was subdivided into 280 residential lots, and home building on the sites began.

Today, the area is called Herron-Morton Place, and the Hedback Theatre is a cornerstone of the community. Staff members at the theater have seen and experienced a variety of hauntings. The stage lights go on and off, strange sounds are heard coming from empty rooms, the strong odor of death and disease comes and goes, and mysterious sobbing has been heard. In one instance, a light on the stage continued flashing on and off, even after it was unplugged. Many of the staff have seen the ghosts of Civil War soldiers in the basement. One in particular makes a routine of walking from one end of the basement to the other without his head. The ghostly soldiers seen in the theater's basement are apparitions from the Camp Morton days.

Julie Powers, an Indianapolis actress, was working on costumes in the old apartments above the theater in 1992 with her two-year-old daughter. It was the middle of the afternoon, and the pair was alone in the building. Looking up from playing, the little girl said, "Do you see the lady, Mommy?" "Where?" Powers asked. "Right behind you, Mommy." When Powers turned around, there was no one there. Having experienced other strange things at the theater, she scooped up her daughter and ran downstairs. In the bright sunlight, Powers felt brave enough to ask her daughter about what she had seen. The little girl said, "The lady was wearing a long black dress and kept talking about her children. She was sad. Oh, and she didn't have a head. Mommy, isn't that funny?" Powers didn't think it was funny; she thought it was creepy.

Powers says that a lot of weird things happen in the second floor of the Hedback Theatre and the connected Epilogue Theater. There is a rumor that a murder was committed long ago on the second floor of one of the theaters. With such a vivid past, filled with misery, sadness, and death, it is no wonder the Hedback Theatre has a few ghosts.

THE ROYAL THEATER

59 S. Washington Street
Danville

Just fifteen minutes outside Indianapolis, in the bedroom community of Danville, sits a little theater on courthouse square. It seems out of place, the Tudor revival exterior sets it apart from the other more traditional brick buildings. But the Royal Theater has been showing movies since 1914. When it first opened, the theater looked much like the other buildings on the square, but in 1926 an Englishman bought the Royal and wanted to bring a little of his country's architecture to the Westside enclave. The Royal Beautiful, as he called the theater, was expanded and renovated, and the new exterior was created. The theater had a steady following for decades but by the 1970s and '80s, attendance had fallen and the theater changed hands several times.

In 1996, the Royal's doors closed and stayed closed until Lee Comer, a local attorney, bought the theater in 2001. He used his own funds to renovate and refurbish the aging theater. The once gleaming walls were repainted, large velvet curtains were hand sewn, and the old wooden floor was covered with concrete. The Royal's interior once again matched its regal exterior.

But the years during which the doors were locked and windows darkened did something to the Royal. The omnipresent loneliness and abandonment was a rich and nourishing nexus for the spirits that resided within. As soon as the night before the reopening premiere, odd occurrences started to happen. Staff readying the theater for the next day's opening were working late cleaning the auditorium. When they were all near the front, a loud scrape and bang came from the projectionist's booth in the back. Everyone was accounted for, no one had been in the booth, and nothing seemed to have fallen. They could not figure out where the noise had come from.

On other occasions, the water faucets in the restrooms turned on by themselves, and light bulbs have frequently exploded. The ghosts of the Royal seem to make themselves known to staff more than patrons. They must save up their energy for after hours or else cannot be heard above the movie soundtracks because most of the haunting stories come from past and present employees.

"The ghosts at the Royal like to sneak up behind you and whisper in your ear," said one former employee. While cleaning the concession area after closing one night, her name was whispered from right behind her. She spun around but no one was there. Shaken, but wanting to finish her job, she continued cleaning. Again her name was whispered from over her shoulder. She said, "That was it. I left in a hurry. But this happened over and over again during the time I worked there. I got to the point I could ignore it or when I was feeling brave, I asked it to speak up."

A few times a year the theater hosts local theater groups, and during a production of *Kiss Me, Kate,* Ryan, a cast member, was working on the sets alone when he heard footsteps up and down the stage and circling around him several times. He tried to ignore the sounds, telling himself it was nothing. The day before, Ryan had made fun of a fellow worker who said she had heard a whisper near the concession stand. He said he didn't believe in the ghosts of the Royal but on that night, he became a believer. Ryan, his mind distracted with trying to tell himself there are no such things as ghosts, dropped one of the set pieces he had been painting. It crashed into another set piece, and they all fell down. From the darkened theater beyond him, laughter rang out—laughter from an empty auditorium, laughter from someone unseen.

Lorri and I visited the Royal with a local ghost group. During our visit, orbs were captured via digital cameras near the projectionist's booth and in the auditorium near the front. Group members got EVP recordings in the concession area and near the front of the auditorium. Most of the sounds were unrecognizable. There were words but they couldn't be made out, except for one. The message was clear: "Get out" was captured by a member near the projectionist's booth.

The former employee who had her name whispered summed up her experiences at the Royal as this, "Even when you were working alone at the Royal, you were never really alone."

CHAPTER 4

The House of Blue Lights

(Lorri Sankowsky)

The House of Blue Lights has haunted the memories of residents on the east side of Indianapolis for generations. The stories have existed since the early 1950s, when eager young men illegally parked on the property with their terrified dates, basking in the eerie blue glow of the mysterious house. The tale is still popular today and is considered more folklore than ghost story. However, strange occurrences at the site have indicated that it might hold some surprises for those inclined to dismiss it.

The story of the House of Blue Lights began with an eccentric millionaire inventor named Skiles Test. Test was born in 1889 to a wealthy family and grew up in a mansion in Woodruff Place, a distinguished upscale neighborhood in Indianapolis. Many community leaders as well as artists and writers called Woodruff Place home. Test had a charmed childhood and did well in school. He was articulate, sensitive, handsome, and well liked. His father died when Test was twenty years old, an event that shook him emotionally and possibly caused some of his eccentricities in later years. Test was left with money, property, and prestige.

At the age of twenty-three, he married his first wife, Josephine Benges, and they moved from Indianapolis to what they referred to as "The Farm," a huge piece of property on the northeast side of the city. As surrounding property became available, Test bought it, gradually increasing the size of the Farm to about seven hundred acres. The property included the present-day neighborhoods of Avalon Hills and Hillcrest. The original caretaker's house was renovated for the Tests, and additions were added as needed, evolving over the years into what is now known as the House of Blue Lights.

Test was a moderate drinker, but he threw outrageous parties and was known as an excellent host, making his own special punch and ensuring that no guest had an empty glass. He didn't like to be alone and was happiest when surrounded by friends and family. He would arrange a schedule so that a different friend visited him every day. Holidays and birthdays were cause for celebration. Amusing and unpretentious, Test welcomed everyone to join in the festivities. Cigarettes, bathtub gin, jazz, and all-night parties kept the house on the hill the place to be in the 1920s.

On the outside, the house was a plain, boxy home, similar to a farmhouse. The many additions and remodels obliterated any grace it had once possessed. But on closer inspection, the marvel of the house became apparent. The exterior walls were completely covered with white, milky glass that never required painting and could be cleaned with a garden hose. Test loved the look of glass in any form, and the living room of his home was lined with glass shelves that displayed his glass collectibles. The shelves were illuminated with florescent lights, which also reflected off the marble and many mirrors in the room, creating a soft bluish glow.

The sunken greenhouse had twenty-foot-tall glass walls, a glass ceiling, and marble floors. There was also a music room that housed a piano and thousands of record albums. A sterling-silver chandelier hung in the dining room, and the kitchen also had walls made of white glass. There were guest bedrooms upstairs, but Test's master bedroom was on the main floor as was his legendary private bath- room. The bathroom walls were covered in the same glass tiles found in the other rooms; however, these tiles were accented with dark red and black. Large mirrors covered every available surface, reflecting the red bathroom fixtures. The shower was oversized and, oddly enough, included a safe. The safe and the mystery of its contents were the inspiration for several unfounded rumors in later years.

The house had a maze of tunnels beneath it that connected almost all the buildings on the property. The out buildings included a gen- erating plant, garages, barns, caretakers' homes, and a large complex for the cats and dogs that Test loved. The tunnels were accessed through several trap doors hidden in and around the property. Because of the narrow, twisting, and turning passageways, those who weren't familiar with the tunnels could become lost in the labyrinth.

The biggest attraction, and Test's most famous invention, was the forty-foot-by-eighty-foot swimming pool. It was one of the first privately owned pools in Indianapolis. One end of the pool was over fourteen feet deep. The excessive depth was needed to accommodate the three-story-high diving complex that boasted four diving boards at various heights. A rope swing was also rigged to the diving complex, enabling swimmers to swing out over and splash into the water. If diving and swinging weren't enough, there was also a two-story-high slide. Test was very proud of another invention, a motorized surfboard. The surfboard worked on a pulley system, allowing guests to surf across the entire pool.

The sides of the pool were lined with concrete steps, so it could be entered at any depth. Solar energy was used ingeniously to keep bathers comfortably warm. A series of pipes drew water from nearby Fall Creek into a group of ten-foot-tall pipes that resembled a stand of bamboo. The sun warmed the pipes and the water inside, which was then circulated into the pool. The water temperature could easily be regulated, even during the predawn hours when Test enjoyed his habitual sunrise swim.

Another fascinating aspect of the pool was that a second pool existed underneath the first one. Invented by Test, it was a clever filtering system encased in thick opaque glass and lit from inside by blue lights. At night, the blue glow from the pool was enchanting. Guests spent long hours lounging in and around the water, sipping drinks, and listening to jazz. Raving reviews about the pool circulated throughout Indianapolis society, and more and more visitors arrived to see it. Test was delighted. To accommodate his many guests, he constructed a three-story bathhouse, complete with a fireplace, full kitchen, dressing rooms, sun deck, glass stairs, and an elevator. The total cost of the building was estimated at forty thousand dollars, a huge sum in those days.

When not entertaining his guests, Test could be found playing with and caring for his animals. The complex that he jokingly called "The Farm" really was a farm, with pigs, cows, and a working dairy. At one time, there were sixteen St. Bernards on the property. Test built separate enclosures to accommodate his dogs and cats. The cat park had small, heated houses, lots of toys, and special feeding devices. At the time of his death, there were more than 150 cats living in the park.

His love for animals was admirable but occasionally it bordered on the macabre. When a pet died, his grieving process had some peculiarities. He insisted every animal receive a proper burial, and he kept caskets in varying sizes stored in the tunnels beneath his home. Before the animal was laid to rest, he would photograph it in its casket, often giving copies to his friends. After his death, several photo albums were found, filled with photos of dead pets. Dogs and cats were the most common, but there was also a squirrel buried with a tulip in a cigar box and a bird with a spray of Lily of the Valley tucked beside it. The animals were all buried in an area set aside as a pet cemetery, with small marble tombstones marking the graves of his favorites.

After twenty years of marriage, Skiles and Josephine divorced. The cause of the split was unknown, however they remained amiable, and she was a frequent visitor to the house. A few years later, there was a short marriage to a socialite named Elsa, followed by another marriage to Ellen Saxon, with whom he had his first child, Louellen. Ellen and Louellen lived apart from Skiles in California, and Louellen was twelve years old before she ever saw her father's home in Indianapolis.

Many happy years passed before the legend of the House of Blue Lights intruded on Test's bucolic life. He was always aware of his own reputation as an eccentric and found it amusing. Inexplicably, rumors and stories of his famous home began to circulate. No one really knows where the stories began or why, as is the nature of rumors, however the stories became more and more gruesome with time.

The most popular tale portrayed Test as an insane millionaire who couldn't bear to part with his dead wife's body. According to the story, he preserved her in a glass casket, dressed in a ball gown and illuminated with lights of blue, her favorite color. There were many versions of this story. Some say that he would move the coffin around the house, placing it beside him as he ate dinner, lying next to it in his bedroom, and tilting it upright in the living room so he could dance around it. People swore they saw him, visible through the glass walls, holding a drink in his hand and swirling and swaying to jazz music next to the casket. Another version is that he secretly kept his wife's body in the earthen tunnels under the home, moving her periodically to different areas in case anyone got suspicious. Others said that Test used the blue lights to attract and imprison his wife's undead spirit and that she remained there, trapped between life and death, going about her daily life and even answering the doorbell.

One of the more gruesome stories involves the legendary pool. Test's wife supposedly plunged to her death from the deck of the bathhouse, falling into the pool below. Her body was sucked into the filtering system and torn to shreds. According to the tale, blood and tissue circulated in the water, encased between the glass walls of the pool, for several days—a sight so horrifying for Test that he went insane.

Test initially found the rumors and stories entertaining, probably because they were so ridiculous, considering his wife was alive and well. He began to feed the rumor mill, allowing the blue lights of the pool to remain on twenty-four hours a day. During the holidays, he strung miles of blue Christmas lights through the trees surrounding his house. He liked them so much that he left them lit all year round. When curiosity seekers approached the house, he graciously gave them a tour of the property and often allowed them to use the pool.

What began as a joke gradually escalated into a dangerous and intolerable situation. Ever increasing hordes of people began to trespass on the property. Teenagers and thrill seekers flocked to the home at night, all anxious to see the glowing blue lights and hoping to catch a glimpse of the infamous dead wife. Unable to cope with the crowd, Test reluctantly had a large fence erected around the property during the mid-1950s. The fence did discourage most of the daytime visitors but at night it only enticed the local teens. It became a badge of courage to scale the fence and venture onto the forbidden property. The bravest of the trespassers even dared to take a quick dip in the pool.

Eventually it wasn't enough to just climb the fence or take a quick swim. Serious vandalism began to take place. Fires were intentionally started in several of the out buildings, burning some of them to the ground. Gunshots reverberated through the trees as the blue floodlights became targets. Drinking and fighting were common among those who used the property as a place to party. Several of Test's pets were hurt or killed. Cats were snatched from the cat park and thrown into the dog enclosure. Dogs were beaten and kicked, resulting in broken bones and lost teeth. The pet cemetery was ravaged, the marble stones either maliciously damaged or stolen as keepsakes.

It no longer was safe for Test to stay in his beloved house, but despite pleas from his friends and family, he refused to leave. He remained there until his death at age seventy-four and was buried in his family's plot in Crown Hill Cemetery. The day after he died, his beloved Farm was taken over by his bank. It immediately closed all access to the property. Family members were shocked to find the once-famous pool unceremoniously drained and surrounded by a fifteen-foot-tall chain-link fence.

Soon, the largest and most famous auction in the history of Indianapolis took place, drawing an estimated fifty thousand people. Most were just curious onlookers but there were also serious buyers in attendance. Included in the auction were cars, jewelry, and furniture. Other more unusual items were also for sale. The miles of tunnels beneath the property had been emptied, relieved of the oddities that Test had so carefully hoarded. For unknown reasons, he had stockpiled thousands of dollars worth of survival equipment along with casks of nails, cases of aspirin, barrels filled with oil, and tiny caskets intended for his deceased pets. The auctioneers were ecstatic, claiming that people paid more per item than any other auction they had presided over. Yet the most sought after item was never found—the supposed glass coffin.

In his will, Test left eighty acres of his property to the city of Indianapolis to be turned into a nature park. The infamous House of Blue Lights was razed in 1978, and the Skiles Test Nature Park was officially opened a few years later. The park has purposely been left in its natural state with no development except for a few dirt trails and a new greenway. It is now home to varied wildlife, including coyotes that can be heard in the evening howling at the moon.

Unfortunately, the park has also attracted some less desirable inhabitants. The urban location, combined with the dense foliage and isolation, has made the park an advantageous meeting place for unsavory characters. Occasionally these incidents turn violent, as in 2003 when police found the bodies of a man and his friend burning inside a Jeep on Fall Creek Parkway adjacent to the park. Vigilance by neighbors and park rangers has greatly reduced such incidents, however visitors should be wary and careful when entering its boundaries, especially alone.

Although public interest in the House of Blue Lights has waned in the past several years, the story has not been forgotten. Retired evening news anchor Mike Ahern still remembers. "Going to the House of Blue Lights was the same as visiting the Tee Pee Restaurant or going to Riverside Park," he says. "It was a rite of passage for Indianapolis teenagers." He never visited the property as a teen but he did broadcast a news story from there shortly before the house was razed. As Ahern and his cameraman slowly wandered through the house and around the pool area, he solemnly said, "Even in the daylight, this place retains a haunted quality." That quality was evident, in spite of the workers in the background busy dismantling walls. The concrete edges of the famous pool were cracked and covered with algae, and the rain water that had collected in it was clogged with fallen leaves. The once-elegant bathhouse looked forlorn and dismal; its iron staircase and façade stripped. Ahern perhaps said it best during the closing of his broadcast: "A crumbling majesty, like a scene from *Sunset Boulevard.*"

Inspired by recent rumors from those who swear they continue to see glowing blue lights in the Skiles Test Nature Park, Keri and I first visited the park on a late evening in August. We were joined by a few members of the Indiana Ghost Trackers and began following a dirt trail deep into the property. One of the other members had a little knowledge about where the house had been located, so we set off to find what we could. After what seemed like miles of hiking, we approached some unnatural topography. Beneath the thick carpet of undergrowth, we found what looked like sewer pipes jutting out of the ground. Further inspection revealed a large slab of white marble. We meandered around for a while, taking digital pictures and EVP occasionally. Eventually we found where we believed the famous pool had been, however it had been filled in with dirt and was now covered with shrubs and young trees. Before we left, we found some small shards of what looked like china or porcelain. One was definitely from a plate or bowl, and it had a thin strip of green decorative paint on it. Another one was a jagged chunk of milky glass, possibly from the exterior walls of the home. I tucked the pieces into my pocket.

Once I arrived home, I removed my muddy hiking boots in the garage, set my ghost-hunting gear on a shelf, and took the two pieces of china from my pocket. Haphazardly I tossed them inside one of my boots and put the boots on the floor in my bedroom closet. Soon, I had completely forgotten the relics that were inside.

Several weeks later, I came home late one evening to find my bedroom closet in disarray, shoes and clothes flung on the bed and on the floor. My husband, Danny, was industriously shampooing the carpet inside the closet and complaining about finding a lot of mud in there. Whoops! He finished the job, hung my clothes back on the rod, and put my many shoes back into the closet. The next day, I was surprised to find the two white pieces of china from the Skiles Test Nature Park lying neatly on the closet floor, as if someone had deliberately set them there. I called out to Danny for him to come and look. "Where did you find these?" I asked him. "I had completely forgotten about them, and why did you throw them on the floor of my closet?"

Danny looked puzzled. "How did you get these back?" he asked. I looked at him, confused, and his face lost its color. After staring at me for several moments, he said, "I found these in your boot while I was cleaning out the closet. I threw them in the bathroom trash and then emptied the trash into the can outside." Yet, somehow they mysteriously reappeared in my closet.

Knowing Danny's proclivity for jokes, especially concerning my ghost hunting, I stifled a smirk and congratulated him on freaking me out. He did not return my smile, but only continued to gaze at the innocuous white pieces of china. It took me a few moments to realize he couldn't have had any idea where I found them or the history behind them. To him, they were just trash I had dragged home, along with the mud.

We speculated on how and why those chunks of china found their way back into my closet but nothing made any sense. It wasn't the dog or the kids. The most compelling evidence that I had was my own husband's reaction. In spite of my experiences while ghost hunting, he remains a steadfast nonbeliever and usually scoffs at the thought of anything I dub paranormal. Here stood the big skeptic, pale, perplexed, and getting cold chills down the back of his neck.

I began to see the House of Blue Lights and the story of Skiles Test in a new way, thinking perhaps there was more to it than just some great folklore. No matter how Test may be portrayed in stories and rumors, the truth remains that he was a gentle, caring, and generous person who was well liked by those who knew him. The notoriety of the House of Blue Lights overshadows this kind and sharing person, leaving me with a disturbing thought. Perhaps this property has not been haunted by Test or his beloved wife, but by the house itself. Whatever the reason, they say the hills of Skiles Test Nature Park still glow with an eerie blue light, visible to motorists on Fall Creek Road and adjacent neighborhoods. When questioned, the neighbors just chuckle and say, "Oh that? That's just the House of Blue Lights." Maybe one dark night, you'll see it, too.

CHAPTER 5

Hannah House

(Keri Young)

Little did Alexander Hannah know in 1858 when he was building his grand twenty-four-room brick Italianate mansion that one hundred years later, his beloved home would become the centerpiece of children's nightmares, cause passersby to cross the street and avert their gaze, and one day be called the most haunted house in Indiana.

Alexander Hannah was born in southern Indiana in 1821, but by 1850, he had made his way west to California to be a part of the gold rush. He never struck gold, but he worked hard and made a good living, owning an interest in a large vegetable ranch. After five years, he had enough of the Golden State and returned to Indiana. Purchasing 240 acres of his father's property in what was then the wild back woods eight miles outside the city of Indianapolis, Hannah began construction on an elegant, red-brick mansion. When the home was completed, he was still a bachelor and lived alone with his servants, but in 1872, at the age of fifty, Hannah brought a bride to his mansion. Elizabeth Jackson would become the mistress of Hannah House and oversee the addition of a summer kitchen, smokehouse, milk house, and servants' quarters.

By all accounts, Alexander and Elizabeth were very happy through the years in their home. The couple never had children. However, some said Elizabeth had a stillborn child that caused her untold grief and pain but was never talked about nor officially recognized. Through the ensuing years, the couple continued to entertain, stayed active in city events, and kept up their many civic associations. Elizabeth died in 1893 and Alexander in 1895.

There were no heirs to Hannah House, so the land and home were

Hannah House

subdivided and sold. In 1899, the home and surrounding acreage were bought by Mr. Roman Oehler, a local jeweler, and upon his death was passed to his daughter Romena Oehler Elder. In 1962, Hannah House was passed down to its current owner, Romena's son, David Elder. The house has undergone major restoration and is now open for social events, weddings, and even haunted tours and overnighters.

The ghost stories started in the mid-1960s after the house had lain empty for more than thirty years. The most famous story of Hannah House involves a noble cause. Alexander Hannah was a fervent abolitionist during the years before the Civil War. It's said that he built a secret room in the basement of his home to hide fleeing slaves on their way north to freedom. Hannah's mansion was a perfect spot for a stop on the Underground Railroad. He owned hundreds of wooded acres with no close neighbors for miles, and wagons arriving in the dark of night would not be seen.

On one of these nights, several slaves were hiding in the secret room in the basement. It was cold and cramped, and the only light came from a single oil lamp. Tragically, the lamp was knocked over, and the dry timber walls caught on fire. The flames raged, and the poor souls trapped in the room were unfortunately bolted in for their own protection. That protection became their death knell. Many perished before Hannah and his servants could rescue them from the blaze. To avoid detection, Hannah had his servants bury the dead in the dirt floor of the basement. In subsequent years, this floor was covered in concrete but its secrets have never been fully revealed. Hiding slaves was not an activity that would have been kept in record books or talked about openly, so there is no absolute proof that this story is true, but it has been passed down from one family generation to the next.

Every once in a while, new evidence pops up lending support to the Underground Railroad theory. One spring day in the mid-1990s, a man came to one of the monthly open houses at the mansion and told Scott Longere, longtime Hannah House manager, about a tunnel he had found. He said he was working on a construction site three streets over from the mansion where they were digging a deep foundation for a new discount store when the crew came upon a tunnel. A few brave workers followed the tunnel as it made its way east towards Hannah House. About a block and a half from the mansion, the tunnel was collapsed, and they could go no further. They followed the tunnel back west as far as they could before that end was collapsed as well. The tunnel was going toward the White River to the west. Nothing was done about the mysterious tunnel. The discount store was built, a parking lot was paved, and most forgot the tunnel ever existed. Could this have been a nefarious secret passage leading to and from the White River, where slaves traveled by boat under cover of darkness, made their way through the underground tunnels, and found themselves at Hannah House's back door? No one will ever know for sure.

Mysterious incidents in the Hannah House basement lend credence to this story. One of the most common ghostly occurrences is the sudden smell of acrid human sweat and fear that is gradually taken over by the strong stench of burning wood. Cold spots have been known to move around the basement, some areas dropping in temperature by as much as twenty degrees. Many people have felt watched and some even touched when walking around the basement.

Through the years, family members and visitors have told of hearing moans and screams late at night, Some echoing so loud as to wake those sleeping on the second floor. The sounds of breaking or crashing glass have been heard coming from the basement. Once it was even heard by two police officers called out to investigate the unusual noises. But when anyone goes to check for the source of the crash, nothing is amiss and no broken glass is found. Those on the first floor have heard loud banging on the floorboards below, bangs that seem to follow those on the first floor from room to room, as if someone wants attention.

The basement is not the only area of paranormal activity in the mansion. The entire house seems to be active. In the first-floor parlor, a large chandelier was seen swinging back and forth by a camera crew filming a segment for a local TV show, and in the same room, minutes later, a large heavy picture fell from the wall. Upon inspection by the shocked crew, the nail had not broken; it was still firmly in place in the wall. The hanger on the picture was not broken either. For this heavy picture to have fallen without breaking the nail or hanger it would have had to be lifted off the nail and then dropped. The crew swore no one touched the picture.

The beautiful carved oak stairway is another active site. A man in a dark suit with mutton-chop whiskers has been seen going up and down these stairs. Never saying anything that adults can hear, the man walks slowly up the stairs and then disappears on the upper landing or walks down and disappears in the front hallway. Children, on the other hand, have been heard talking to him.

During a Halloween bonfire and cookout held at the house with staff, family, and members of the Indiana Ghost Trackers, Sarah Kennedy's five-year-old daughter, Maddie, came into the house via the back porch and into the hallway near the stairs. Pointing, she said, "Mommy, there is an angel on the stairs." But Sarah didn't see anyone; the stairs were empty. Or were they?

When the house is quiet, the rustling of a woman's long skirts can be heard through the long hallways, as well as the sound of high-heeled shoes tapping on wood, even on areas long ago carpeted. Off the second-floor hallway is a door to the attic that is always locked because its stairs are dangerously steep and the door will not stay shut. The tightly locked attic door is known to burst open with cold gusts of air when no one is visible around it. This is such a common occurrence that there is a warning sign on the outside of the attic door asking visitors to stand clear.

Longere says that the door is not the only paranormally active part. The whole attic is paranormally charged. When he is in the attic to make repairs or to bring stuff up for storage, he feels like someone is watching him from the far corners of the room. Sometimes that feeling of being watched is accompanied by the sound of low whisperings of words he can't quite make out. But what sends a chill down his spine and sends him back down the stairs in a hurry is that, every once in a while, he can make out his name among the whisperings.

Longere recounts another incident that took place in the attic. He was in the attic with a few people from a haunted tour. Two men on the tour had dowsing rods and were walking the attic with them, looking for any sign they might register magnetic or spirit energy. The dowsing rods crossed or pointed to activity near Longere. Suddenly a blue ball of light appeared an arms length from Longere's face. As he looked closer, this blue light took on the shape of a man's face. It was semitransparent; he could see through it but could still make out the features. Longere said, "I didn't recognize the face. I was so shocked I really couldn't even signal to the other people what I was seeing. I am startled by things in this house, but not frightened by what's here. I think they just want to make their presence known."

The second most famous haunted spot in the mansion is the upstairs back bedroom. Many stories about this room have been written, some based on fact, some purely fiction. The most popular story is that Elizabeth Hannah had some medical problems while pregnant and sadly lost her child in this room. The stories go on to say that this room has the smell of death that no amount of soap or bleach can erase. A few psychics who have visited Hannah House for various events have stated they felt a pregnant woman in a great deal of pain in this room but could give no further information.

There are no records of a child's death associated with the house, but at the Hannah family cemetery plot in Crown Hill Cemetery, there is a small, unmarked gravestone between those of Alexander and Elizabeth. It is the size of stone that was commonly used for infants. Longere adds that, "Most of the psychics that visit the mansion have problems with [the back bedroom]. Some get physically ill and have to go downstairs, saying the energy is too strong for them. Others state that the tremendous energy draws them to the room."

Another popular story is that this was the room used by Mrs. Oehler in her later years after she had become bedridden and in which she eventually died. Previous occupants of the house have stated that they would sometimes smell something rotten like decaying flesh or death in the room, a smell they could not scrub away with bleach. Alternately, they also smelled roses, even in winter. It can be confirmed that Mrs. Oehler died in the room, in the very bed that remains there to this day. The owners today say they have never smelled anything rotten or decaying and cannot confirm that these smells have ever existed. However, they and I have smelled the pungent sweet smell of roses when no visible flowers were around.

Lorri and I first investigated the infamous Hannah House with the Indianapolis chapter of the Indiana Ghost Trackers. During this time, Hannah House and the Indy IGT developed plans to have a ghost-tour fund raiser that would help to offset the tremendous upkeep and tax costs for this privately owned National Historic Registry property. In order to have plenty of scary tales to tell the customers, the group spent many nights investigating the property and gathering paranormal evidence.

On the first investigation, approximately ten Indy IGT members, including Lorri and I, gathered at the mansion at 10 P.M. We separated into groups, evenly distributed between the three floors, and began setting up our equipment. Lorri and I joined the group that started in the basement. We took preliminary readings for temperature and looked for sources of explainable electromagnetic fluctuations before we set up our meters. The group split into pairs, and Lorri and I started doing EVP around the perimeter of the basement. We asked questions such as, "What year is it?" "How did you die?" and "Did you have any children?"

After the investigation, Lorri and I played back the tape, and in one spot of the basement, the eerie, cryptic words "Find me" were spoken loudly and clearly over the conversation we were having. We were alone in that corner of the basement when this was recorded.

The back bedroom on the second floor of Hannah House is thought to be haunted by the former lady of the house or a deceased child.

Others in the basement were getting temperature drops of unexplainable origin and pictures on digital cameras of orbs of varying sizes at the same time

Upstairs, group members were getting digital images of orbs in various rooms throughout the house. A motion detector was placed on the second floor outside the attic door, and then the floor was cleared. All gathered on the first floor for a debriefing and to go over any evidence gathered so far. Fifteen minutes into the debriefing, suddenly the motion detector started blaring. The attic door, although not locked, was left shut when the group left the floor. It was now wide open, and something unseen had tripped the motion detector.

After the investigation had wrapped up, Lorri's teenaged daughter, Caitlin, and her two friends wanted a private tour of the attic. With only one flashlight, Lorri ascended the creaking narrow stairway, leading the teens into the dusty, dark attic. When they reached the attic floor, the door below suddenly swung shut with a loud bang. Lorri later noted, "It seemed to grow colder, and we could see our breath. I cursed myself for not bringing the IR thermometer with me.

A burst of wind hit the house, causing the old ceiling beams to creak and moan, and just then the flashlight flickered and went completely out. I smacked the flashlight with the palm of my hand and it fluttered back to life, weak but emitting enough light for us to see the stairs. Quickly we descended, only to discover that the door had not only slammed shut but was also stuck." Lorri had the kids bang on the door and call for help. Meanwhile, she went back up to the attic to try to get someone's attention through the windows. With no luck, Lorri started to climb back down the stairs when she heard a shuffling and scraping sound coming from the dark far corner of the attic. Not wanting to scare the kids, she ignored the sound and continued to descend the stairs. The kids asked her what they were going to do, and at that moment, the dragging and scraping sound came again, this time at the top of the stairs. When Lorri didn't think she could take it any longer, the door popped open, and they all spilled out onto the second-floor landing. Lorri said, "I slammed the door shut and clicked the padlock. The entire door felt like it was made of ice." They went downstairs to join the others, and the teens had a good story to share with friends.

On another investigation night, two Indy IGT members, Amy and Chris Garrison, were investigating the basement. They were doing EVP and began discussing that six months earlier Lorri and I had recorded the words "Find me" in the basement. When they played back their audio tape later, right after that mention, a voice out of the darkness faintly says, "Find me" again. Someone not of this earth wants to be found in the Hannah House basement. It's not a coincidence that EVP taken six months apart produced the same pleading cry for help. The mystery is, who wants to be found.

From another spot in the basement, Amy recorded the words, "Go up." Chris and Amy have investigated Hannah House many times, and we asked them for a few of their other paranormal stories. Amy said, "While a few of us were investigating the library, we were taking digital pictures and doing EVP recordings. A compass that had been set up to try to catch fluctuations suddenly started acting up, the dial spinning to the right and then back to the left. EVP taken near the compass recorded a faint, quick 'Keep away'." Amy goes on, "During the fund raiser, we had a group down in the basement, and we were telling stories about the activity in the basement. A blue lantern start-ed swinging back and forth on its own. I went over and stilled the lantern and asked that whoever did that, could they do that again. In front of everyone, the lantern started to slowly swing back and forth."

On another trip to Hannah House, Lorri and I interviewed Scott Longere about his experiences through the years at the house. He told of one night he and Elder family friend Sharon were in the kitchen cleaning up after a wedding. Longere said, "My cell phone started ringing." "I looked at it, and the caller ID said Sharon's phone was calling. Sharon was sitting right in front of me with no phone. She had locked her purse and phone in the pantry. She unlocked the pantry, got out her purse and phone, and saw that her phone had called mine several times that night."

Later that night, Sharon told us of a window in the upstairs front bedroom that will not stay unbroken. She took us upstairs and pulled back the curtains, the large front window was taped together with duct tape. She said, "We replaced this window not a month ago, and yesterday I noticed it was broken again. This window has had the glass replaced more than ten times in the past ten years or so. And the weird thing is, the glass is always broken from the inside out."

Paul, an Elder family member, told of a night when he was doing some repairs inside the house alone. He happened to glance out the front windows and saw someone on the front porch pacing back and forth. It was late, and the house's reputation attracted a lot of kooks and those trying to show their bravado. Paul picked up the first solid object he could find and opened the front door, ready for a confronta-tion, but there was no one there. There had not been enough time for someone to have run away unseen. Paul says he often wonders if it was the ghost of Alexander, checking on his beloved mansion.

Scott Shepherd, another family friend, was working at the haunted house event, which was a local tradition in Indianapolis during the 1980s. He had stepped outside on the back porch to take a smoke break when he saw a man moving through the trees in the side yard of the property. He and another volunteer called out to the man. The man didn't respond so they walked toward him. "He was right in front of us. We tried to jog up to him, and right as we got to him, he disappeared."

At a monthly Indy IGT meeting, several members presented

evidence gathered on investigations at Hannah House. A member that had investigated the house many times and had volunteered during the Haunted Overnighters at the house had some significant evidence to present. He said he tried an experiment in the basement. He took a blank chalkboard, rubbed chalk over it, and spoke out loud to any entities that might be around that he wanted to communicate with them through the chalkboard. He showed them how to mark in the chalk dust by drawing a circle and a line through the chalk. He left the board in a corner of the basement and went upstairs to continue his investigation. Hours later, he and another IGT member went down to the basement to see if anything had been produced. Amazingly a faint backwards *C* had been made in the upper part of the board, and the beginning of a *J* had formed in the lower bottom left corner. As the two members looked at the board, the *J* began to grow larger right before their eyes. They couldn't believe what they were seeing and called more witnesses to take a look. Four members saw the astonishing *J* being formed on the chalkboard. The member brought the chalkboard to the meeting, and we were able to see the faint letters drawn in chalk dust.

With all that has been seen and heard in Hannah House and all the evidence that has been collected, Lorri and I think that Alexander, Elizabeth, and maybe others are still walking the halls of their beautiful home.

CHAPTER 6

The Indiana State Fair

(Lorri Sankowsky)

The Great Indiana State Fair, a Hoosier tradition for more than 150 years, is an odd place to look for ghosts in Indianapolis. It is the sixth oldest state fair in the United States, with a rich history of harness racing, agriculture, and entertainment. The fairgrounds are located in a most unusual, urban area, surrounded by the inner city at the intersection of East Thirty-Eighth Street and Fall Creek Parkway. Trailers full of livestock wheel down Thirty-Eighth Street alongside pimped out automobiles blaring hip-hop music, the exhaust fumes competing with the aroma of fresh manure.

The state fair began in 1862 and was held in what is now Military Park. It changed locations a few more times before settling permanently at its current address in 1892. Development and improvement continues today, making it one of the premier fairgrounds and event locations in the country. The fair is a place of fun and family, but underneath the laughter of unsuspecting guests there is an undercurrent of dark calamity. Like a spoiled jar of blue-ribbon pickles, a nasty thread of accidents and deaths mar the friendly façade, culminating with the greatest tragedy in the history of Indianapolis.

Even in its infancy, the state fair seemed to be a place that inspired wonder as well as horror. In 1869, the Sinker and Co. saw mill steam boiler was drawing crowds of curious bystanders, eager to see the newest innovation in technology. As people craned their necks to watch the boiler in action, it suddenly exploded, showering the crowd with shrapnel. The engineer and several onlookers were killed instantly. Doctors and nurses rushed in to care for the injured and dying, using burlap feed sacks as makeshift bandages. Twenty-four people were killed, and several dozen were seriously hurt in the first but unfortunately not the last tragic loss of life.

Racing and auto sports have always played a large role in the history of Indianapolis, and the state fair saw a lot of action on its oval track. The dirt-packed track stretches east to west, totaling one mile. It has hosted everything from harness racing to demolition derbies to sprints. One of the most beloved acts to ever appear on the dirt oval was the Hell Drivers. These auto daredevils performed heart-stopping stunts that entertained fairgoers for many years.

On a hot July day in 1942, twelve thousand people crowded into the grandstand to watch Earl "Lucky" Teter and his Hell Drivers perform. Boldly colored leaflets promising "The Most Reckless, Fearless Men Who've Ever Lived—Defying Death at Every Turn of the Wheel" had lured the huge crowd. The advertising did not exaggerate. As spectators fanned themselves under the broiling sun, they were treated to motorcycle stunts, dangerous stock-car racing, and several deliberate collisions. The drivers remained miraculously unscathed and bowed to the appreciative crowd.

The grand finale was Lucky himself, a pioneer in the sport of auto stunt driving. He was the only driver who performed the Daring Leap. After charging up a ramp at high speed, he would sail 125 feet over a parked truck to another ramp, landing safely on the other side. Lucky was solemn as he spoke to the crowd that blistering afternoon. He was scheduled to be inducted into the armed services the following day and proudly announced this would be his last jump until after the war. He also dedicated his last stunt to "not only the soldiers here, but to all the boys in Uncle Sam's armed forces throughout the world." The dust from the dirt track hung heavily in the humid air as he gave the crowd a jaunty wave and entered his car. As Lucky stomped on the accelerator and approached the ramp, mechanics raised their heads with alarm as they heard the motor miss. The car never reached the speed necessary to propel Lucky up and over to the waiting ramp. His tires skimmed the parked truck in the middle of the jump before the nose of his car plummeted and he crashed into the exit ramp supports. The ramp collapsed, and Lucky was crushed. He was killed instantly.

The dirt track claimed another victim a few years later. The

Indianapolis Auto Racing Association sponsored a one-hundred-mile race in 1946, which later became known as the Hoosier Hundred, one of the most prestigious races in the history of dirt car racing. Unfortunately the race was marred by an accident so horrible that former and eventually re-elected Governor Henry Schricker declared that cars would never again race on the track as long as he was in charge. During a practice lap, Indianapolis driver Al Putnam skidded and slammed into a concrete wall between turns three and four. Track employees scrambled to pull him from the crumpled car, however their attempts were futile. The steering column had pierced his chest, pinning his lifeless body to the steering wheel.

Residents of the closely packed neighborhood on the edges of the fairgrounds often hear the sounds of racing engines during the night. When the wind is blowing a certain direction, a whiff of engine exhaust is carried on the breeze, even in the dead of winter. The ghostly drivers are still racing through the darkness to a finish line in eternity.

Not every ghost roaming the dirt track has such a morbid beginning. An enthusiastic racehorse named Greyhound also haunts the area. Appropriately, his nickname was the "Grey Ghost." He made racing history during the Great Depression, inspiring millions of people with his great speed and elegant stride. His silvery-gray mane and tail whipped through the air like a silk scarf as he flew around the track, amazing onlookers and breaking speed records. As a colt, Greyhound was just an average horse. Nothing about him foretold the riches that he would earn later in his life. He was awkward, lazy, and tended to be bad tempered. Seeing no future for him, his owner had him gelded and sent to an auction in Indianapolis where he attracted little notice and was sold for nine hundred dollars.

Greyhound's life changed when he became the responsibility of three men, his new owner, Colonel E. J. Baker, trainer-driver Scepter Palin, and caretaker Jimmy Wingfield. This trio saw potential in their new horse, and neither money, time, nor kindness was spared for his training and care. Scepter Palin, more commonly known as "Sep," became a beloved figure in the history of horse racing, and together he and Greyhound shattered speed records, the majority of them on the dirt track at the Indiana State Fairgrounds. He set a total of twenty-five world records between 1934 and 1940, some of which are still standing. In 1941, Colonel Baker decided to retire Greyhound from competition. The horse still appeared at racing events, adorned in a shiny red harness, his silver coat gleaming. He would prance before his adoring fans in a parade lap, regally nodding left and right, acknowledging their applause. In his later years, he retired to luxurious quarters where he attracted daily visitors. His guest book was signed by thousands of people, some of whom traveled from the far ends of the earth to see him. At Christmas, he would receive hundreds of gifts from school children. Every day he was walked outside to an apple orchard, where he happily scratched his back against his favorite tree, nibbled on apples, and rolled in the soft grass.

Greyhound lived to an astonishing age of thirty-three. Although he became thinner and suffered from a touch of arthritis, his health remained good until his death on February 4, 1965. His old friend, Colonel Baker had preceded him in death. However, he had left provisions to arrange for Greyhound's remains to be shipped back to his beloved Red Gate Farm, where he was buried.

Yet Greyhound's adventures do not end with his death. Some say that a horse this legendary never sleeps, and a few people know this for a fact. They say that Greyhound's ghost returns to his old stomping grounds at the state fairgrounds and kicks the walls of his old stall. It happens most often following a momentous occasion in the horse-racing world, as if Greyhound is celebrating the victory, too. It is described as the sound of a spirited kick, nothing spooky or ethereal—a nice solid thud.

The horse stables are on the east side of the racetrack, and the first one is aptly named the Palin Barn. Visitors who go there find a large, dusty stable, filled with stalls, harness equipment, and a few horses. The barn is still in use today and bears a large plaque commemorating Sep Palin.

The day Keri and I investigated the barn, it was dry, dusty, and hot. As we entered the cool darkness of the stable, it felt almost like walking into a church. Sounds from outside seemed muted, and we found ourselves whispering, almost reverently. The comforting smells of leather, hay, and horses were like an expensive perfume. I breathed in deeply and was immediately comforted; reminding me of the long hours spent grooming my aunt's regal horse, an Arabian named

Darrack. The present owner of the stable said she had never experienced anything ghostly herself but graciously showed us the stall that had once been Greyhound's home for many years. It was now used for storage and had not sheltered a horse for a long time.

The dust in the barn made any kind of photography useless; all the photos appeared to have hundreds of orbs. Instead, we decided to try recording some EVP. I held the recorder while Keri took temperature readings and also monitored our compass. Not sure what kind of questions to ask a horse, I whispered his name. Several minutes went by with no reaction from either the compass or the IR thermometer. Feeling a little stupid, I said his name louder. Looking helplessly at Keri, I shrugged. What exactly do you ask a ghost horse? Finally, as we were getting ready to leave, I said, "Greyhound, are you here?" The silence was shattering. Even the other horses stood quietly, as if they too were listening for an answer.

Later that evening, we played the tape recording. I felt a little embarrassed as I heard myself struggling on the tape, trying to communicate with an animal. Cringing, I continued to listen until the very end, when I loudly asked, "Greyhound, are you here?" There was a long pause, and then I heard it—a solid kick. The sound of a shod hoof clearly striking wood. We were thrilled to know that the "Grey Ghost" was not only still haunting the stable but also seemed to have a sense of humor.

The Coliseum at the fairgrounds has showcased a variety of big-name entertainers and was the home for the Indiana Pacers for several years. Wrestling brought huge crowds during the 1960s and 1970s. Patrons watched in awe at the ring antics of Dick the Bruiser, Wilbur Snyder, BoBo Brazil, and Cowboy Bob Ellis. Boxing, hockey, and ice-skating were also big draws. Unforgettable entertainers who appeared at the Coliseum include Bob Hope, Johnny Cash, Nat King Cole, Michael Jackson, Willie Nelson, the Beatles, and Elvis Presley.

No one will ever forget the rainy Halloween night in 1963 when death made an unwelcome appearance. That date will live in infamy as the worst tragedy in the history of Indianapolis. It was opening night for "Holiday on Ice." The skaters glided gracefully across the ice in sparkling feathered and beaded Mardi Gras costumes, performing their grand finale in front of a sold-out crowd. At the concession area, located behind aisle thirteen, a stealthy hiss of propane, used to warm popcorn, was leaking undetected from a faulty valve. At 11:04 P.M., the propane ignited. An explosion ripped through the side of the arena, lifting seven hundred square feet of occupied seats upward and onto the ice. Chunks of steel and concrete crushed spectators and performers. A few seconds later, another blast rocketed upwards, followed by a thirty-foot wall of flame that burst from the crater.

Bodies flew up and out of their seats, landing on the hard ice, some nearly sixty feet away. Lighting crews, stationed on platforms anchored high above, reported bodies flying up in front of them, illuminated by the colored floodlights they were using. The band assumed that the noise was part of the pyrotechnics and continued to play Dixieland jazz, unaware of what was happening. Men and women began frantically running in every direction, their clothes melting onto their skin from the heat. Blood and body parts littered the aisles, and those who could move quickly stampeded for the exits.

The explosion created a pit fifty feet wide filled with huge masses of concrete, steel girders, and dead bodies. The fire continued to burn at the bottom. The smell of charred flesh haunted rescue workers for years afterward. Some of the remains were so badly burned that recognition could only be accomplished through dental records, not a very reliable source in the early 1960s.

No one in the city of Indianapolis was prepared for such a mass-casualty incident. Not only were there dead bodies to deal with, but more than five hundred people had sustained injuries. The wounded were left behind as hordes of panicked people streamed out of the building, creating a barrier that prevented the incoming firefighters and rescue workers from getting inside to battle the blaze and care for the injured. Rescue operations were further delayed as the state and city battled over how to control the scene. In a scenario that is a grim precursor of the September 11 tragedy, all civil communication and organization broke down. Ambulances that were able to get through the stalled traffic were directed to take their passengers to only a couple of the city's many hospitals, creating chaos and stretching the limits of their emergency personnel. Other hospitals hastily primed their emergency rooms for a full-scale disaster but never received any patients.

Family members and the media converged on the fairgrounds desperate for information, impeding the early stages of the rescue efforts. Agencies duplicated emergency procedures while more necessary ones were never initiated.

When it was over, sixty-eight people lay dead and eight others would die in the days that followed. Bodies had to be extricated from the tons of rubble. The frozen ice rink was littered with bodies that had adhered to it and had to be carefully scraped off. The ice did have one advantage; it was used as makeshift morgue. Bodies were placed on plywood and then lined up on the ice according to gender and age. Family members had to walk through the rows of charred and dismembered bodies to identify their loved ones.

The explosion remains the worst tragedy in the history of Indianapolis, and those who work and play in the concourses, aisles, locker rooms, and snack bars of what is now known as the Pepsi Coliseum say a few of those who died so suddenly and tragically are still there. Unexplained cold spots are reported in different areas, and several people have reported seeing a middle-aged woman in a long coat seated next to aisle thirteen, looking out toward the arena. Blink and she's gone.

Late at night, lights flicker on and off and passersby on their way to their cars have seen movement inside the glass doors, although the building is locked and empty. The smell of smoke permeates the air with no apparent cause. Employees were reluctant to speak with us, however

After a tragic explosion, the floor of the Coliseum was used as a temporary morgue. Photograph courtesy of The Indianapolis Star.

an older person who wished to remain anonymous, spoke of an experience when working late one evening. "This feeling just came over me; I don't know what caused it. It was like someone had just walked over my grave. One minute I was fine, and the next I was awful scared, even breaking out in goose bumps. I just left, it was that scary."

Keri and I visited the Coliseum on several occasions, however the nature of the building does not bode well for ghost hunting. The acoustics prevent any useable form of tape recording, and the size and draftiness prohibit recording temperature changes. The EMF meter went off every few seconds, picking up on the electrical equipment that is wired through the walls and aisles. After failing with so many methods, we decided to take a seat along aisle thirteen and just wait to see if anything would happen.

Settling into our seats, we kept the compass where we could easily see it and switched on the tape recorder, just in case. It wasn't long before the dark arena began to play tricks with our eyes. There seemed to be sudden flashes of color that appeared in the corners of our eyes but disappeared when we turned our heads. Shadows of gray morphed into solidity, only to dissipate when focused upon. We looked at each other and laughed nervously, not quite sure if we were seeing anything paranormal. The muffled sound of traffic from Thirty-Eighth Street waned in and out, and we began to hear a sound underneath it, a stealthy clicking noise, like the sound of a ballpoint pen being tapped along a steel pipe. The clicks were sporadic, without any discernable rhythm, occasionally pausing for long moments and then resuming, louder than before. I quietly spoke into the darkness, "Is someone there?" The clicking came to an abrupt halt. We waited, expecting the sound to resume again, but it did not.

At that moment, I began to realize that I was hot. I mean, really hot. The air in the arena had been almost chilly when we first arrived, and I was wearing a light jacket. I shrugged it off, thinking perhaps the heating system had been turned on, but our IR thermometer showed no rise in temperature. Beads of sweat broke out on my forehead, and I began to feel flushed. I noticed that Keri also had removed her coat and was fanning herself unconsciously with her notebook. "I am burning up!" I told her. She stated that she also felt overly warm, and we checked the IR thermometer once more. It had

not changed from the sixty-seven-degree reading that we first recorded. The longer I sat there, the more uncomfortable I got. Soon, I had
sweat dripping from my bangs, and my shirt was sodden. I couldn't
concentrate on anything other than my unpleasant physical state.
Finally I announced that I couldn't stand it anymore, and we gathered our equipment and walked out onto the concourse. The temperature there seemed normal, cool against my hot skin. What the heck?

I handed my things to Keri and marched back into the arena and
returned to where I had been sitting. The temperature remained cool,
almost drafty, and I was taken by a sudden chill. Slowly the hair on my
scalp began to rise, and I broke out in goose bumps. Shadows of gray
seemed to swirl around my head, and a wave of dizziness caused me to
grip the handrail. Enough was enough, and I fled back onto the concourse. Despite this, we were able to obtain a picture with a rare red
orb floating in the area where the spectral woman normally appears.

Judging from our experience there, the ghosts of the Coliseum are
active and not so welcoming. They also seem very protective of aisle

*A red orb is visible in a photograph of the area in the Coliseum near aisle thir-
teen, where the ghost of a woman has appeared.*

thirteen. Visitors to the Coliseum might be lucky enough to catch a glimpse of them or perhaps the other ghost that reportedly haunts the arena. I can't vouch for the accuracy of the reports but I would be remiss if I didn't mention the most famous ghost sighting in the dark hallways. Allegedly bathed in a pale blue light and dressed in a sequined suit, the ghost of Elvis Presley has been seen silently meandering, his head bowed, through the shadowy concourses of the Pepsi Coliseum.

CHAPTER 7

Eat, Sleep, and Play . . . With Ghosts

(Keri Young)

Cemeteries and haunted houses are the first places people think of when they want to find ghosts. But from our experiences, ghosts can be found just about anywhere. This chapter explores the fun side of ghosting—restaurants that boast more than excellent cuisine, hotels where you can share a room with an unseen roommate, and places to have fun with a ghostly flare.

EAT
THE MILANO INN

231 S. College Ave.
Indianapolis

In 1934, Joe and Mary Modaffari opened the Milano Inn Italian restaurant on the near east side of downtown Indianapolis. Through the years, the Milano built a solid reputation for excellent southern Italian favorites and a welcoming atmosphere. A steady stream of neighborhood regulars filled the parking lot around the two-story red-brick building until closing every night of the week. The Milano thrived for more than four decades in the Modaffaris' skilled hands but upon their deaths in the mid-1970s, the restaurant passed to family members who just didn't have the same flare as Mom and Pop Modaffari and business started to decline.

To the rescue came Leo LaGrotte, owner of a neighboring railroad-equipment salvage business. He took over the building, and after extensive renovations and the hiring of a new chef, the Milano Inn opened back up for business with the bonus of northern Italian favorites added to the already extensive menu. The combination of upscale interiors and an expanded menu brought the regulars and newcomers back in droves.

During the renovation, LaGrotte expanded the restaurant by tearing out the old abandoned apartments on the second floor and adding banquet rooms. The renovation did more than add square footage to the restaurant; it unleashed something that had been lurking in that space, unnoticed and waiting for years.

"We don't like to be alone upstairs when we have to clean up late," one staffer said. "It feels like you are never alone and always being watched." Other staff members have mentioned flickering objects that appear and disappear just beyond full view and dark shadows that move in the hallways behind the bar. Whistling, glass crashing, and footsteps have all been heard in the empty upstairs rooms.

A psychic that visited the Milano said she felt that Mary Modaffari was still looking over her beloved restaurant and that she is the one watching over workers, moving things around, and showing her disapproval if she thinks anyone is slacking off.

There is also another explanation for the haunting. A staff member said, "Many years before the building was a restaurant, a young lady named Mary lived in one of the apartments upstairs. One night a terrible fire struck the upper floor of the building. Mary tried to get out by the landing door but it was warped from the heat. She banged on other doors and called for help but no one answered her. The flames were beginning to shoot across the ceiling, and Mary panicked. She threw herself against the landing door, which still wouldn't open, and a flame near the doorway caught her long nightclothes on fire. Those on the street outside could see Mary, her gown in flames, running from room to room looking for help. She then disappeared, not to be seen again. She was overcome by the heat and smoke and died in the fire."

When a local ghost group visited the Milano to do an investigation, they found evidence that poor Mary is still wandering the last home she knew. They got several EVPs with whispers that can't be made out, the sounds of choking, the name Mary, and a faint female voice saying, "It hurts." A member reported feeling her throat closing up, smelling smoke surrounding her, and feeling faint in the smaller back banquet room.

Lorri and I visited the Milano on several occasions with a ghost group and on our own. We found no activity on the lower level, but upstairs was another story. After the last diner had left and we had the floor to ourselves, we began our investigation by setting up equipment in strategic areas. We put two motion detectors on either side of the floor and placed a TriField natural EM meter in the smaller banquet room. Taking digital photos, I got several large orbs in the main banquet area and the area around the back spiral staircase. As I was showing Lorri the photos, one of the motion detectors started blaring.

When we inspected the area, nothing around the detector was disturbed. Lorri went off to ask the staff if they happened to walk by the detector, and I went to adjust the setting on the other motion detector. When I had turned the corner, the motion detector went off again. This time I hurried back but saw nothing. As I approached the detector, the hairs on the back of my neck started standing on end. The area was freezing cold, so I grabbed the IR thermometer. The thermometer registered sixty-two degrees. I didn't have an initial reading from that exact area, but the general temperature upstairs had been a steady seventy-five degrees.

Later that night, Lorri and I were sitting in the small banquet room doing an EVP session. After a while, Lorri noticed the subtle smell of smoke. It grew stronger until it could be smelled all over the small room. It was not an overpowering choking smell, but similar to the lingering smoke smell after a campfire has been extinguished. We looked for the source of the smell from the kitchen, then downstairs and outside. We couldn't find the source. At the end of the night, we compared all the evidence gathered. We had gotten meter readings, orb photos, temperature drops, tripped motion detectors, and the smell of smoke. We did not get any EVP.

For a paranormal experience, visit the Milano and ask to be seated upstairs. You just might get more than meatballs for your money.

ROCK BOTTOM RESTAURANT & BREWERY

10 W. Washington Street
Indianapolis

Today, 10 W. Washington Street houses the Rock Bottom restaurant and brewery. Known for its home-brewed ale and superb burgers, Rock Bottom is located on the same block as the location of the infamous Bowen Merrill Fire. In 1890 a terrific fire raged that ultimately claimed the lives of thirteen Indianapolis firefighters and is considered one of the worst fires in Indianapolis history.

In 1861, Silas Bowen opened the Bowen Merrill Co. one block south of Monument Circle in a four-story building on West Washington Street. The popular stationary and bookstore had a steady, brisk business, and the building's basement housed the extensive paper products the store sold. On a beautiful St. Patrick's Day afternoon in 1890, a worker went down to the basement to pick up an order and noticed a plume of smoke rising from a corner of the basement. That plume soon gave way to a roaring fire as employees shouted for everyone to get out of the building. The fire department was called, and eventually every available unit in the city would be fighting the raging fire fed by the reams of paper stored in the basement.

By five o'clock that evening, the entire building and its contents were almost entirely consumed by the flames. The interior of the building was too hot for firefighters to enter, so a hole was cut in the roof to get water directly to the burning core. As dozens of firefighters stood atop the building, the roof gave a thunderous shudder and then suddenly collapsed inwards, taking with it many of the firefighters. Panic ensued, and spectators and fellow firefighters rushed to try to save those who had fallen inside the burning building. Trapped men could be heard screaming from underneath piles of rubble and brick. A few lucky ones were dug out quickly and given medical attention; others could not be located and their screams finally faded away.

After all were accounted for, thirteen firefighters lost their lives in the Bowen Merrill fire—eleven on the day of the fire and two soon after. The citizens of Indianapolis donated more than thirty-five thousand dollars to the relief program for the widows and children of the firefighters, and Crown Hill Cemetery donated burial plots. Most were buried in Crown Hill on March 20, 1890.

Rock Bottom is known for its spirits—the hops kind—but it just might be known for the ghostly kind as well. Customers playing

A memorial sign marks the location of the deadly Bowen Merrill Fire of 1890.

pool late in the evening have told stories of the sudden smell of charred wood and soot surrounding them. In the ladies room, the faucets turn on by themselves. One long-time waitress said sometimes the staff sits around the bar after closing sharing a beer or two before heading out for the night. On one of these occasions, a loud crash came from downstairs. They rushed down but no one was there. Staff members have had their names called when no one is around, glasses behind the bar are constantly breaking, patrons have felt an icy hand on their shoulders or arms, and cold spots develop all over the restaurant. Servers say that they catch a hint of the smell of smoke throughout their shifts, but it becomes really strong after all the patrons have gone home for the night. I asked some of the servers if the activity increases on St. Patrick's Day, the anniversary of the fire. They said they couldn't tell. "Its so crazy with people celebrating the day and drinking large amounts of Guinness, the ghost firemen themselves could walk in and they would be given a beer and not noticed." Rock Bottom needs further investigating—perhaps with a pitcher of green beer.

SLEEP
EMBASSY SUITES – DOWNTOWN

110 W. Washington Street
Indianapolis

Klingons, not ghosts, were on the minds of Gen Con convention-eers David and Kim when they traveled to Indianapolis from Milwaukee for the largest annual science fiction and adventure game convention in North America. But when they choose the Embassy Suites – Downtown as their overnight accommodations, they got more than a place to bed down. They got a poltergeist.

One night, the couple came in from a late dinner and found things amiss in their room. Things were not where they had left them. Kim said, "I always put the toothpaste next to the sink, and when I went to use it, I found it in the tub. And my hairbrush was in the trash. I know I didn't do that. The key ring was not on the dresser but on the floor. Small things like that were out of order, but we put it down to the maid cleaning up and went to sleep.

"About 3:00 A.M., we were shocked out of sleep by a crashing sound in the bathroom. David got up and flipped on the light. All the stuff on the counter had been thrown to the floor: make-up, soaps, curling iron, hair dryer, everything. We were a little freaked out and kept the bathroom light on the rest of the night. If it hadn't been our last night, we would have gone to another hotel."

After hearing Kim and David's tale, I went to the hotel to ask some of the employees if they had experienced anything paranormal. The front-desk folks said they had never heard of anything paranormal at the hotel, but then most front-desk employees say that. The banquet wait staff had a different story to tell.

One long time employee said that he knew of several guests who had checked out in the middle of the night for mysterious reasons. A few had actually said it was because they knew a ghost was in the room with them or that they felt uncomfortable, like someone was watching them in the hallways and rooms. Another employee said that she felt watched when cleaning up late at night or delivering room service to the seventh floor. She said, "I really don't like the seventh floor. I don't know why, but it gives me the creeps. Sometimes, when it's late and I have to deliver something to that floor, the hairs on the back of my neck stand on end." I asked if anyone knew who or what was haunting the Embassy Suites – Downtown, but they didn't know for sure. They said it could have something to do with the old hotel that used to stand on the same block as the Embassy.

In 1852, the Victorian-style Bates House was built at the corner of Illinois and Washington streets, the same spot the Embassy Suites – Downtown now occupies, offering rooms to weary travelers for the grand sum of two dollars a night. The hotel hosted high-profile guests, most notably, president-elect Abraham Lincoln, who made a speech from the Washington Street balcony. When the Bates House was demolished after a decline in business, the grand Claypool Hotel was built in its place in 1901. At eight stories and more than five hundred rooms, it was the grandest hotel in the Midwest.

The Claypool boasted a theater, assembly hall, ballroom, rooftop garden, and cafés. It had the prestigious distinction of having more bathrooms than any other hotel in the country. The opulent hotel attracted the famous and powerful, and because of its proximity to the Indiana statehouse, it became a popular place for legislators and housed both the Democratic and Republican state headquarters.

But all was not golden within the walls of the Claypool; there were murders committed in its gilded halls. On August 28, 1943, Corporal Maoma Ridings checked into room 729. But by eight o'clock that same evening, housekeeping would find Corporal Ridings slashed to death, lying in a pool of her own blood on the floor of her room. The only clue the police uncovered was the sighting of a mysterious woman in black who called for room service from room 729 around 6:30 p.m. The busboy could not say for sure if it was Corporal Ridings. The official finding was that Corporal Ridings was killed by a blow to the temple from a whisky bottle. The same broken bottle was then used to sever her jugular vein and gash her wrists, neck, and torso. The authorities never discovered who committed this heinous crime, and the murderer was never caught.

A decade later, on a July morning in 1954, the badly decomposed body of eighteen-year-old Dorothy Poore was found stuffed in a dresser drawer in room 665 at the Claypool Hotel. Her family told authorities she had gone to the city to see about a job at the Claypool. It is not known if she spoke with anyone at the hotel or how she ended up in room 665. The man who was registered in that room had given a false name and disappeared. A hotel blotter from the Kirkwood Hotel was found by an *Indianapolis Star* reporter in room 665, which led police to the real identity of the man. Victor Hale Lively had registered at the Kirkwood under his real name, and the police were able to piece together the clues that put Lively not only in the Kirkwood, but in room 665 of the Claypool on the night Dorothy was murdered. Lively was apprehended in St. Louis, brought back to Indianapolis for prosecution, and ultimately convicted and sentenced to life in prison.

It's not known if the tragic deaths of these unfortunate women are the cause of the paranormal happenings at the Embassy Suites – Downtown today, but their tales are tragic enough to have imprinted themselves upon the fabric of time.

CROWN PLAZA HOTEL AND CONFERENCE CENTER AT UNION STATION

123 W. Louisiana Street
Indianapolis

America's first Union Station holds many secrets. After passenger train travel fell out of fashion in the 1970s, Indianapolis' Union Station closed its doors to passengers forever. What was once a bustling station with more than two million passengers a year became a ghost town—literally.

Night watchmen patrolling the area tell stories of seeing ghost soldiers silently walking the deserted tracks in the dead of night and the sound of whistling that comes out of thin air. Abraham Lincoln's death train has been seen on the anniversary of the date it passed through Union Station in 1897, rumbling silently, with no one on board alive.

Indianapolis' first Union Station was built in 1853 but the rapidly growing popularity of train travel made it necessary to construct a larger building in 1888. Five hundred thousand passengers a month traveled through the new red-brick and granite Romanesque revival building for destinations all over the country. But by the late 1970s, train travel had been outpaced as the popular form of transportation. Union Station closed to train traffic in 1979. That same year a mall was incorporated into the station. For a while, it did very well, but the transformation of Indianapolis' downtown brought a death knell to commercial use of Union Station. After 1997, the station was closed and abandoned.

In 1986, the Crown Plaza Hotel bought the abandoned train shed of Union Station and renovated it to make a one-of-a-kind hotel. It rolled in thirteen authentic Pullman train cars on tracks one through eight and literally built the hotel around the cars. Guests can spend the night in a real train car. All twenty-seven train car rooms are named after celebrities and dignitaries from the early 1900s and offer the same amenities as the traditional rooms. When guests check in they receive a sleep mask and ear plugs and are cautioned to not be alarmed by any rumbling they might encounter. Tracks ten through twelve are still operational and run just to the south of the hotel, close enough that you can feel the slight vibration if you are on that side of the hotel.

In 1999, the Crown Plaza bought Union Station's Romanesque revival main building and renovated it for its grand hall and conference center. The thirteen-thousand-square foot grand hall retained Union Station's soaring stained-glass barrel ceiling, detailed arches, revival-style columns, and corridors filled with the largest collection of antique Rookwood tile in existence. On either side of the hall, identical twenty-foot hand-crafted leaded stained-glass wheel windows help make this one of the most sought after locations for weddings, banquets, and parties in the city.

Ghost people are scattered around the hotel and conference center but these apparitions are made of fiberglass. Artist Gary Rittenhouse created twenty-eight life-sized "ghost people" statues dressed in authentic period clothing and carrying items from their times. But some say the statues don't like to stay in place. Hotel staff members have reported that guests and sometimes new staff members will frequently come up to the front desk and ask if the statues are on wheels because they swear they have moved. One guest who had a statue of

a traveling sailor outside of his room went to bed and woke up sometime in the night. He said he heard talking in the hallway and opened
up his door to tell whomever it was to be quiet. There was no one
there but then he noticed the sailor seemed to be a few feet from
where he remembered it being before he went to bed.

The Pullman train cars are said to be a source for hauntings at the
hotel as well. Guests staying in the train cars have heard the whistle
of a train, felt the wheels moving, and smelled coal and fumes as if
they were on a moving train. Some have awakened in the night swear-
ing they heard a conductor calling "All aboard" and issuing instruc-
tions to the crew. Some have felt the icy touch of someone in their
rooms, and in the darkened space between train cars, shadows and
figures have been seen lurking about.

I wanted to investigate these stories for myself so I checked into
the hotel and was given the Jean Harlow train car for my overnight
investigation headquarters. Taking digital photos in my train car, I
didn't get any orbs or other phenomena. The train car rooms at the
Crown Plaza are still on the original tracks. Two side-by-side trains
are lined up, and each car has two guest rooms. When my niece,

*An orb appears in a photograph of one of the Crown Plaza Hotel's
"ghost people" statues.*

Taylor, who had joined me for part of the investigation, and I took photos in the dark space between the two trains along the tracks, we immediately started getting orbs of differing density. Some were far off down the tracks, and a few were within inches of our faces. I immediately got out the tape recorder and started an EVP session. I went up and down the train cars with the EMF detector, but no disturbance was detected.

Later that night, I asked a room-service steward if he had heard of any ghosts at the hotel. He spoke in a soft whisper saying he had personally seen ghosts on two occasions. He said he had been delivering room service to the Rudolph Valentino train car late one night when he noticed a man walking towards him from the other end of the hall. He kept glancing up from his tasks because there was something off about the man. As the man got closer and closer, the steward could see that the he was staring intently right at him. He had a dour expression on his face, and the steward braced himself for a confrontation with an unhappy guest. Right then the guest in the Valentino car opened the door, and the steward momentarily looked away from the other man. When he turned back around, the man was nowhere to be seen. The steward left the Valentino car guest waiting for his food as he searched the hallway for the man. He never found him.

"On another occasion," he said, "I was making sure that the doors at the end of the hallway that lead to the outside walkway to the RCA Dome were locked one night. The doors are right by the caboose trains. It was dark and quiet, and then I heard a terrible noise. The only way I can describe it is it sounded like an angry bull was charging me. I heard heavy breathing, panting, loud movement, and an angry roar or snort. I didn't see anything but then I had run as fast as I could back out of that hallway. I got another worker, and we cautiously went back to that hallway. All was quiet. I try to avoid that end of the hallway now."

Back in my room, I laid down on the bed to play back the EVP session. Gently I felt the rumblings of a train going by. Most of the recording revealed nothing, but in a few spots there is a shuffling sound and low muffled voices. I can't make out any words, but I do think I captured murmurings that were not heard by my ear when I did the taping. When I was checking out I snapped a few quick digital photos of the white ghost figures of a man getting a shoe shine from a boy in the lobby. A dense orb appeared near the little boy in the photo. I showed it to the front-desk clerk and said, "I think you might have spirits here." But as every good front-desk person will do, she ignored my comment and said, "Have a nice day."

IVY HOUSE BED & BREAKFAST

304 N. Merrill Street
Fortville

Jim and Linda Nolte have lived peacefully in their Fortville home for more than thirty years. In 2000, after their children left the nest, they decided to fulfill a life-long dream and opened Ivy House Bed & Breakfast. Ivy House is a stately but welcoming Dutch colonial, situated on the highest point in Fortville, a suburb of Indianapolis about twenty minutes northeast of the city. Lacy carpets of ivy blanket the grounds. The inside is filled with gleaming antique woodwork, offset beautifully against tones of rose and sage. Built in 1921, it was originally the home of physician Jesse Ferrell. Dr. Ferrell was known to have other interests in addition to healing the sick. He loved to gamble and bet on the horses. Construction on the home had to be halted at one point because he had gone broke gambling, but he eventually gained enough funds to finish the house.

Gambling seemed to be the theme of the early years of Ivy House. There were rumors of mafia involvement and tales of black sedans that lined the driveway, waiting to drop off dark and mysterious passengers for a night of gaming. Another source claims to have met the infamous mob leader Al Capone during one such night at the home.

Over the years, the Noltes have found various gambling-related items in the home. Punchboards were found in the insulation. In the attic, they were amused to find the floorboards were made out of portions of old gaming tables. The basement had also been used in Dr. Ferrell's time to store illegal gambling machines, such as one-armed bandits, or slot machines.

Regardless of the possible gangster activity and elusive gambling that might have occurred in the home in the past, the Noltes had never experienced any paranormal activity in the thirty years they have lived there. But the arrival of a player piano changed that forever. The piano had originally been in the home next door, which the Noltes also own. It had been left there by an elderly woman who didn't have the resources to move it when she left. They don't know any of the history surrounding the piano, only that strange things began to happen once they placed it in the corner of their living room.

"We were downstairs in our family room," Linda said, "and we heard someone walking through the living room upstairs. I knew no one should be up there so I ran up the stairs, and there was no one there. This was right after we moved in the piano." The phenomenon continued. "Over and over and over, the footsteps would walk across the floor. We would just swear that someone was up there, but there never was. Once our daughter came to visit and told us that someone was walking upstairs. We told her there wasn't anyone there. She was skeptical and went to look herself. When she came back down, she couldn't believe it. We now call it our piano ghost." The ghostly footsteps are heard so frequently that Jim and Linda seldom go upstairs to investigate them anymore. "We have motion detectors in the driveway and the front door," Jim explains. "If we don't hear the motion detectors go off, we don't bother going up there."

Because the piano originally resided in the house next door, Jim and Linda asked their neighbors if they had experienced anything unusual while the piano was in their home. "We were kind of joking about it at first," Jim said. "We told them what had happened to us from the first day we moved the piano into our home and asked them if they had ever had anything happen while it was in theirs." The couple stated that they had never had anything unusual happen, when suddenly, in the middle of their discussion, the electricity went out. "It was like a disturbance in a thought process. Everything went black," Jim said. It only lasted a few seconds but it was enough that they had to reset their computer and their TV. The strangest thing is that we are all on the same transformer, so if their power went out, our power should have gone out. When we got home, all of our digital clocks and computers were fine. Our power hadn't been interrupted. After that, we were really convinced that something was going on."

A guest at Ivy House told the Noltes that she felt the presence of a ghost in their home. Linda explains, "There were two couples who came together, and they were standing at the top of the stairs, looking into the Boston Ivy Room. One of the ladies suddenly turned and asked me if we had a ghost! I laughed and told her about the piano ghost. She said that the ghost she felt was of an older woman. The ghost was very sad and looking out of this window." The window Linda pointed to faced west and was covered with lacy curtains.

"The people who lived in this house before us are still in this area, and we ran into them recently," Jim continued. "They told us their grandmother had lived in this room. She was sad that she had to leave her old home, which was just around the block, and frequently looked out this window to see it. We don't know if she is connected to the piano or not." The Noltes are more bewildered than bothered by their piano ghost. They don't know why it's there or what brought it, but they accept it graciously into their beloved home and offer guests the chance to stay in one of their comfy guest rooms and try to find out for themselves.

PLAY
ACTION DUCKPIN BOWL

1103 Shelby Street
Indianapolis

Most people have never heard of duckpin bowling. But the little-known sport is all the rage at the Fountain Square Theatre just south of downtown. The Fountain Square Theatre is the heart of the up-and-coming eclectic-arts and cultural enclave of Fountain Square. Built in 1928 as a grand movie and vaudeville show place, the ornately decorated theater could seat 1,500 guests. For decades it was the Southside's premier entertainment venue. But the 1950s saw a decline in grand movie palaces, and Fountain Square was no exception. Interest waned, and the theater was sold and gutted to make room for a Woolworth's five and dime.

The entire Fountain Square commercial district took a hit when many residents were displaced by the building of a new interstate in the 1960s. Woolworth's and many other retailers closed their doors. The Fountain Square Theatre building saw tenants come and go with long stretches of empty storefronts. In 1993, the present owners bought the building and started renovations that would bring it back to its glory days. The theater building now boasts a hotel, an original 1950s soda fountain and diner left over from the Woolworth's days, a 1,500-seat theater, an upscale bistro, and two vintage duckpin bowling alleys.

The unusual sport of duckpin bowling started on the East Coast in the early 1900s. At that time, regular bowling was only played during the winter months. Hard-core bowlers were itchy during the off season, and a creative alley owner in Baltimore came up with the idea of playing during the off months with a much smaller ball, smaller pins, and different rules. He had a six-inch wooden ball created and had regular pins whittled down to match the size of the ball. The much harder game caught on with bowlers, and the sport took off. As its popularity gained, the game was played year round and not just as a replacement league in the summer months.

Indianapolis is more than eight hundred miles from the East Coast, but in 1994, during the renovation of the theater building, the owners installed an authentic 1930s duckpin bowling alley on the top floor of the building. Action Duckpin Bowl has eight lanes for regulation duckpin bowling, a 1918 pool table, an extensive collection of vintage bowling memorabilia, and a café. But the owners of the theater building thought one alley of duckpin bowling was just not enough. On the lower level of the building, the Atomic Bowl features seven duckpin alleys, and a 1950s theme, juke boxes, pool tables, and a soda fountain add to the atmosphere. But some say there are more than pins rattling around the theater building.

There are things happening in the bowling alleys at night. Sometimes workers set the pins on the lanes the night before if they have a reservation for the next day. Eerily, when the workers come back in the next day, all the pins have been knocked down as if a game has been played on the lanes overnight.

On one occasion, the staff had finished cleaning up the lanes, turned off the lights, and headed downstairs to leave. One staff member remembered she had forgotten something up on the fourth floor in the Action Bowl area. When she ran back upstairs to retrieve it, she got the shock of a lifetime. She rode the elevator up, and when it hit the fourth floor she exited the elevator into the dark hallway. As she got closer to the door to the bowling area, she heard what sounded like a party on the other side of the door. She heard laughter, glasses and plates clinking, and the sounds of the small balls going down the wooden lanes. She didn't want to open the door but she had to. She got up the nerve, opened the door, and all was silent and dark. No one was there, and no balls were in play—silence. She ran in, got her forgotten item, and ran out of there as fast as she could.

Another staff member told me that there are ghosts in the hotel part of the building as well. One night the security guard was doing his rounds on the hotel floor. He had just walked down the hall and was about to get on the elevator when he heard the sounds of high heels clicking down the hallway behind him. He turned around quickly to see who was there, but there was no one. Suddenly he realized the hallway was carpeted; high heels could not have made the clicking sound on this surface. The staffer thought it was the ghost of the lady that many of the staff have encountered. "She wears fancy clothes and probably high heels. Her blonde hair is pulled up, and she always looks sad. It's probably her, clicking down a hallway that in her day was not carpeted. I've seen her in mirrors, and once, in the theater, I saw the misty outline of just her bottom half. The apparition stopped at her chest; she didn't have a head or shoulders."

Lorri and I were not able to do extensive investigating at this site, but we did get a large amount of orb photos in the theater area. If the management becomes more agreeable, we would like to go back to the Fountain Square Theatre for further investigating.

BOGGSTOWN CABARET

6895 W. Boggstown Road
Boggstown

In the unfortunately named little town of Boggstown, there is a theater with as much drama going on after the last curtain call as during the production. The two-story brick building was built in 1873

Boggstown Cabaret

for the state's first Red Man's Lodge, a national men's club.

Throughout the years the building has housed a barber shop, men's athletic club, and Boggstown's General Store. In the 1960s, the upper floors were converted to apartments, but in 1984 the entire building was taken over as the Boggstown Inn and Cabaret. During these years, shows featured dueling pianos, ragtime, comedians, and banjo music in a casual setting. In 1999, the cabaret came under new ownership, and the name was changed to the Boggstown Cabaret. The interiors were updated to resemble the famed supper clubs of the 1920s and '30s. Today's shows feature detailed costumes, music, drama, and comedy. But after the lights go down and the last diner has left, the cabaret takes on an otherworldly feel.

Julie Powers, entertainer and public-relations director for the theater, says it is definitely haunted. "The staff and even some customers have had numerous run-ins with the paranormal here. The wife of the previous owner was the first one to see the little-boy apparition.

One night she walked around the corner downstairs, and there was a little boy standing by the ice machine. She went to speak to him, and he just disappeared. After that, he has been seen by diners and staff on many occasions throughout the years, but we can't find any record of who this little boy might be."

Powers has seen the apparition of a man who came into her dressing room. "I thought it was Randy, our previous comedian, but when I turned around to look at him, no one was there." There are also cold spots and footsteps that echo all over the theater. The footsteps are especially loud going up and down the back stairs, but when that area is checked no one is ever there. The batteries for the alarm system that surrounds the theater are often dead. Technicians have been called out but they can never find a cause.

Lights go on and off when no one is around, and the light booth itself is a scary place. Powers says, "In the light booth, you can feel someone walking up the stairs; it shakes a little. But when you get up and look out the door, no one is there." "Ghosts also like to lock the doors," she said, "When I am performing, at a certain point in the production, I have to go out one door that leads outside and enter from another door. I always check that these are unlocked before the performance. Some days the doors would be unlocked at the beginning of the performance but when it got time for me to exit, the door would be locked or the other door back inside would be locked. I have gotten locked out of the building during a performance. Finally I told them to stop, and they did."

The upstairs has its ghosts as well. There are still some bedrooms from when it held apartments. A musician playing the theater for a week spent his nights in one of these rooms. Mysteriously, one night he left in the middle of the night. When Powers finally got a hold of him, he said he heard the piano downstairs playing ragtime music all by itself and decided that was enough for him. Powers said, "People who sleep upstairs tell us they see shadowy figures moving around all night and people walking around downstairs." A waitress that had gone upstairs to use the ladies room came running downstairs half dressed. She said the shower curtain in the bathroom had opened and closed with no one there.

Powers went on, "A lady from Boggstown told me her son had

lived upstairs when it was apartments in the 1970s. She said her son told her the place went crazy one day. Furniture moved around by itself, pictures fell off the walls, dishes crashed to floors. He said he had to literally crawl out of his apartment."

Powers doesn't have any answers as to who might be haunting the theater but the staff thinks there are at least three spirits there, that of a little boy, a man, and a woman. She also says that certain seasons seem to have more paranormal activity. "They like the fall and when we are especially busy. They seem to like a full house. Once, when we were in the middle of a packed show, a heavy glass exploded on the table in front of a guest. When we remodeled, the heavy bad feeling that was sometimes felt went away. Now it feels better, more playful and benign." At the Boggstown Cabaret, mysterious knocking, footsteps, exploding glasses, ghostly piano music, and apparitions come with the ticket price.

CHAPTER 8

Ghostly Graveyards

(Lorri Sankowsky)

Graveyard. Cemetery. Why do these words spark an involuntary shiver in many people, a tiny dose of uneasiness? Why are cemeteries feared, avoided, and referred to in hushed tones? Do we really feel the dead will rise from their graves, blindly grabbing at our ankles with

Main Street Cemetery at twilight

dirt-encrusted fingers? Or do the weathered stones etched with the names of those long deceased painfully remind us of our own mortality? Is our unreasonable fear rooted in adolescent memories? Raising our feet off the floorboard and holding our breath until our car passes safely by the wrought-iron fences. The haunting face of Sammy Terry glowing eerily from our grainy black-and-white television. As the host of *Nightmare Theatre,* he terrified three generations

Sammy Terry. Photograph courtesy of Sammy Terry.

of Indianapolis viewers, rising from his coffin every Friday night to introduce a spine-tingling creature feature. The view from the window of his cardboard dungeon revealed a misty Technicolor graveyard where werewolves howled, witches cackled, and corpses came alive.

"There is nothing on this planet as fearsome as a cemetery," says Sammy, also known as Bob Carter. His voice is still unmistakable in spite of his seventy-plus years. "The eerie quiet, the fog rising from between the tombstones. Do you really know who is in those graves and what horrible secrets they hide?" Winking and smiling his trademark sly smile, he chuckles and I have a sudden urge to clutch my pillow and turn on all the lights. "The graveyard is the best place for your imagination to have a horrible good time."

There are huge modern cemeteries throughout Indianapolis. Several of them have very beautiful tombstones, chapels, and crypts in addition to gardens and ponds. Lovely as these parklike places are, they don't evoke the raw emotion eternally captured in the smaller pioneer and family cemeteries that are tucked away and mostly forgotten. Urban sprawl has swallowed an unknown number of these tiny plots, but thanks to restoration efforts a few remain intact, lovingly tended by those who realize their importance. Many of them are located in remote and hidden areas and have suffered greatly, either from neglect or vandalism. To protect and preserve their integrity, the exact locations of the cemeteries that are covered in this chapter are not listed. I would be remiss if I did not include a cautionary reminder to future ghost hunters that all cemeteries are closed at dusk, and permission must be granted to gain access to them after dark. If you are lucky enough to obtain permission, it is my hope that you will repay this kindness by joining in restoration and preservation efforts. The Indiana Historical Society often gives workshops on cemetery preservation and is a good place to start.

Why do ghosts haunt cemeteries? This question is widely debated. Some ghost hunters say that ghost hunting in a graveyard is useless, that a spirit would not choose to linger in the place of its physical remains. Others argue that grief and emotional turmoil charge the atmosphere with energy; spirits feed from this energy, making them more likely to appear at a grave site. Another opinion is that our physical remains continue to "vibrate" with our energy long after our deaths, and a spirit can draw upon that energy to manifest. Almost all the cemeteries that Keri and I have investigated have displayed some kind of phenomenon. Orb photos, unusual EMF readings, and temperature fluctuations are the most common phenomena experienced.

HEADY CEMETERY

Heady Cemetery is a serene and picturesque cemetery located in a neighborhood north of Indianapolis. The Heady family were pioneers who settled in the Fishers area. The cemetery is not especially well known, but an adjacent area has gained notoriety as Heady Hollow. Motorists who know the legend rush through the intersection of 126th Street and Allisonville Road with downcast eyes, fearful of catching a glimpse of the ghostly Heady Hollow children. Reportedly, a tragic fire erupted in a school house run by the Heady family in the late 1800s, killing several children. On foggy nights, the children are said to rise from their graves and appear in the middle of the road, staring coldly at approaching cars. As cars draw nearer, the children dissipate into thin air. The phantom children have been blamed for cars veering suddenly off the road in an attempt to avoid hitting them.

Heady Hollow is not only haunted by ghost children but also by the restless spirits of long-ago travelers who were robbed and murdered while traveling from Noblesville to Indianapolis. Allisonville Road was a direct route for wagons and carriages, and the Heady Hollow area was heavily wooded and often layered with thick fog, providing an ideal spot for bands of thugs to waylay unsuspecting voyagers.

A harrowing story revolves around a once lucrative endeavor—grave robbing. In the mid-1880s, the medical field was desperately in need of cadavers for scientific research and study. The idea of donating one's body to science was unheard of, so alternative methods became necessary. Many medical students were asked to either provide their own cadavers or hire a body snatcher to get one for them. Grave robbing became highly profitable, and an isolated cemetery like Heady provided privacy for those looking to cash in on fresh bodies. Ebenezer Heady was rumored to have been a legendary grave robber. Under the cover of darkness, deep in the woods of Heady Hollow, he met with doctors and medical students, exchanging newly buried corpses for top dollar. Eventually Heady paid for his crimes when he unknowingly exhumed the body of his own son. Upon realizing what he had done, he went mad and lived the rest of his years in the surrounding forest, screaming maniacally until his death. It is rumored that if you listen closely, his tortured screams can still be heard as his restless spirit wanders among the trees.

Keri and I have investigated Heady Cemetery many times. The level of activity there could be described as slight. We have never encountered any ghostly presence, and the cemetery's inclusion in this book was not likely until an event that took place in the late fall of 2007. Based upon the temerity of the legends surrounding Heady Hollow, we decided to make one last visit. The cemetery has an eerie quality at nightfall, as thin fog seeps over it from the adjoining lake. However spooky it appeared, we obtained only minor orb photos and a couple of temperature fluctuations that were probably caused by the dips and rises in the topography. We did not attempt any formal EVP by asking questions, but we did leave the tape recorder on as we did our investigation. Disappointed with our results, we left around midnight.

A few days later, I popped the tape in the tape recorder and decided to give it a listen before discarding it. I was completely flabbergasted by what I heard. Our conversation was almost completely drowned out by the sound of a crow cawing. There were no birds visible to us that night, and we certainly didn't hear anything. The crow's cawing rose in decibels, screeching so loudly that our voices could no longer be heard. As it reached a crescendo right before the tape ran out, it can only be described as a harsh prolonged scream. Perhaps it was the wild ravings of Ebenezer Heady.

DOTY CEMETERY

There is a pioneer cemetery on an isolated bluff overlooking Lick Creek near Fortville. This quiet and secluded spot has provided us with some terrifying moments. It is the family plot of the Doty family, who settled in the area in the 1820s. Research has yet to discover any legends or folklore about the area, only that is was a popular hunting and fishing spot for Native Americans. There were a few Native American and pioneer skirmishes during this time, but we are unsure who haunts the cemetery and the surrounding woods. Our investigations have revealed a high level of activity, and late one night, an incident occurred that made a lasting impression on a future ghost hunter. The Doty Cemetery is tucked far back into a dense forest. It is only accessible via a half mile hike on a rough path, through a stream, over several fallen logs, and then up a rigorous bluff. Keri and I found ourselves on this path in the late fall, accompanied by some fellow ghost hunters and a handful of newbies. The sounds of insects and wildlife surrounded us as we made our way through the thick trees. The path was made even more treacherous by the bounty of fallen leaves that practically obliterated it. We had to backtrack a few times before finally reaching the top of the steep bluff. The cemetery lay before us, small, eerie, and lonely looking in the moonlight.

The tombstones were so old that most of them weren't legible. We examined them carefully, running our fingers over the mossy and pitted stones. The noise in the forest ebbed, waned, and then abruptly stopped. The branches that had been creaking and swaying in the wind were silent; even the cicadas had stopped chirping. It was disturbing and unnatural, as if the volume had been muted in a nature movie.

The sudden silence was unnerving. We looked at each other and laughed timidly. There was a feeling of anticipation; the forest waited expectantly for our next move. A resounding snap startled us, as if someone had stepped on and broken a tree branch beyond the cemetery fence. We stood quietly, eyes wide and all senses alert, waiting to see what would emerge from the trees.

Nothing moved, not even the wind. After a few moments, we looked at each other and laughed nervously, trying to shake off the uneasy feeling. Slowly we started to unpack our equipment. We had barely begun when a loud *CRACK!* came from directly behind me. I jumped, fumbling for my tape recorder, which eventually fell from my clumsy fingers into the grass. I whirled around to see nothing but the wire fence. Flashlight beams revealed nothing but trees and brush.

My stomach began to flutter, and my heart pounded. Although I consider myself psychically challenged, whatever sixth sense I do possess was screaming at me to leave that place immediately. It was as if I were being propelled out of the cemetery against my will. The hair on my neck and arms felt electrified, and my fingers and cheeks were icy to the touch. To my great relief, someone else suggested that we leave. I'm not embarrassed to say that I made quite sure I was not the last one through the cemetery gate.

It was during our hike back through the forest when things got really weird. We slowly picked our way down the path, trying not to slip on the leaves and mud. A big mossy log had fallen over the trail, and we had to navigate over it without getting too filthy or breaking anything. Matt Mooreman, a novice ghost hunter, was walking ahead with some friends as Keri and I straddled the log, chatting and laughing at our efforts. After a few minutes, we were safely back to our cars.

It was much later that evening when I heard what had happened at the site of that fallen log. At first, Matt was reluctant to tell anyone what he had seen. "I turned around to make sure Lorri and Keri made it over the log," he said. "And that's when I saw it. I can't even describe it." Matt's voice quivered slightly, and he admitted that he doesn't even like to remember that night. "Standing beside Lorri on the edge of the trail was the shape of a big burly man. I couldn't make out his clothes but I could see the figure. He was really built, like someone who works out a lot, muscular. He also had on a hat with a wide brim. He was facing me with his hands on his hips and was staring right at me. I could see his eyes; they were shining in the dark." Pausing and shaking his head, he said slowly, "I don't know what it was or what it wanted, but its eyes were boring into me, and I will never forget it". Matt went on to tell me that he had turned away, thinking his eyes were playing tricks on him. "When I looked back again, he was still there, staring straight at me, right into my eyes."

I asked him if he felt that the figure was menacing or if he felt like it meant to harm him. "I don't know," Matt continued. "But I do know that I'll never go back there again, not anywhere even close to it. I always thought this ghost hunting thing was a big joke, and the truth is, I never believed in it, still don't. But, I won't go ghost hunting again either because, if that *was* a ghost, I don't want any part of seeing something like that again."

Matt's story became even more interesting. When our group met back up at our cars, a second group decided to make the hike up to the cemetery. At this time, Matt had not yet told anyone what he had seen. When the second group came back, approximately an hour later, they were talking excitedly about their experience. They had also heard the isolated cracking noises and described the cemetery as being shrouded in fog, although no fog was present when our group had left it. The fog and unnatural quiet of the forest were interesting, however they were overshadowed by the rare sighting of an apparition near a fallen log—a large dark shadow wearing overalls and a big hat.

CROWN HILL CEMETERY

Crown Hill Cemetery lies in the heart of Indianapolis and has the distinction of being the third largest nongovernment cemetery in the United States. It was listed on the National Register of Historic Places in 1973. The wrought-iron fences enclose more than 555 acres. Twenty-five miles of paved roads meander through more than one hundred different species of trees. It is the final resting place of some of the most prominent citizens in Indianapolis history and includes a national cemetery, mausoleums, and historic Victorian-style structures such as the Gothic Chapel.

The cemetery was established in 1864 as Greenlawn Cemetery amid a forest so deep and obstructed that it was only accessible via the river. The center of the property was originally a swamp known as Round Pond and was home to slithering reptiles and panthers. Bears made their dens near what is now the intersection of Thirty-Eighth Street and Fall Creek Parkway. Eventually, the marshy ground was filled in, snakes, bears, and other hazardous wildlife were driven away, and roads were developed. As the city grew, so did the cemetery, and additional acres were added, including the hill that resulted in the eventual name change to Crown Hill. The hill was originally called Strawberry Hill because of the strawberries that were once cultivated there by its former owner. It was a popular picnic spot for the townspeople.

Today, Crown Hill is a source for local and state history. Its residents include some of the most beloved, famous, and infamous citizens of their time. Some of the more illustrious names to be found carved in stone are United States President Benjamin Harrison, Colonel Eli Lilly, author Booth Tarkington, former owner of the Indianapolis Colts football team Robert Irsay, automobile manufacturer Frederick Duesenberg, and the great poet James Whitcomb

Riley, whose monument is perched at the very peak of Crown Hill and is sprinkled with pennies by those who visit it daily. The most infamous character to be found in Crown Hill is notorious bank robber John Dillinger. The location of his grave is still the most often asked question of cemetery employees, and it is the frequent recipient of various tributes such as shotgun shells and empty liquor bottles.

In spite of the size and quantity of graves at Crown Hill, very few ghost stories exist. This could be attributed to the strict observance of a 5:00 P.M. closing time and the vigilant night watchmen who patrol the grounds thoroughly and do not tolerate any nonsense. Another reason could be that the cemetery is still in operation and will be accepting new burials for many years. Employees steadfastly refuse to discuss any type of paranormal activity in deference to those who may be future customers.

In spite of their perseverance, a few stories do exist. One story took place many years ago and involved a night watchman. He was an intelligent and faithful employee who had worked at the cemetery for more than twenty years. In his many years of service, only once did he experience what he concluded to be a paranormal occurrence. It was a very dark night, and he was patrolling the cemetery on foot, carrying a lantern and accompanied by his dog, a collie named Shep. Shep always walked a few paces ahead of the watchman during their nocturnal rounds, nose to the ground and tail wagging. On this particular night, Shep, who had been casually ambling along, came to an abrupt halt. As the watchman stared at him quizzically, Shep carefully moved aside as if he were allowing someone to pass by him on the path. A few moments later, the watchman felt a warm breeze gently float beside him. He fumbled with his lantern, holding it high above his head to illuminate as much area as possible, but the path was empty. The watchman said he knew at that moment that he was not alone. Another soul was also strolling through the graves that night.

Many stories have been told about visitors who have been inadvertently locked in the cemetery after dark. There is one documented case from the early 1900s involving a woman and her small baby. She was unfamiliar with the cemetery and somehow could not find an exit. She desperately cradled her crying baby as the sun set and the cemetery plummeted into darkness. She stumbled aimlessly through the grounds until she found the iron fence that edged the northern end of the cemetery. On the other side of the fence was a road. The road, which is now Thirty-Eighth Street, was remote, dark, and deserted. Eventually, a few travelers did pass by but when they heard the woman's wails coming from inside the foreboding and fenced cemetery, they bolted away as quickly as possible. No one was brave enough to investigate the frightening screams. The woman and her baby were finally discovered the next day, tired, cold, and frightened but unharmed.

Keri and I have been lucky enough to investigate Crown Hill after nightfall. This was a rare opportunity, and we were very fortunate. The cemetery is so big that we limited ourselves to certain areas, concentrating on the Riley memorial, the family plot of the Test family, and the grave of Alexander Hannah, builder of the infamous Hannah House. Perhaps the conditions weren't just right that night or the areas we chose were not active. Although we tried various methods and employed several different pieces of equipment, we never obtained any results worth mentioning. It was extremely disappointing, and we have no idea why this historical place, filled with so many graves, refused to surrender any dark secrets that night.

MAIN STREET CEMETERY

Main Street Cemetery is bad. Those who are buried there are not at peace. A casual afternoon walk through the crumbling tombstones is often marred by a feeling of unease, a sense of wrongness. Even those who are unaware of its infamous history can perceive the unnatural pall that lingers over it like a fetid haze.

Main Street Cemetery, also known as Hays Cemetery, is located in a forlorn, rural section of Hancock County. The nearest home is at least a quarter mile away. Encircled with waving rows of corn, it can only be seen from the road for a few short months after the harvest. There is a wooded area behind it, and the north side lies along a steep ravine. During the summer, it slumbers quietly, out of sight from the rare passing motorist. To reach it, you must walk a rutted and often muddy quarter mile of dirt road.

This road, engulfed by trees and choked with brush, is known as Thomas Road. It has had its own stories of paranormal activity, equally as infamous as the graveyard to which it leads. At the point where Thomas Road penetrates the cemetery, there are two huge boulders that flank each side. According to legend, these boulders surreptitiously move and are never found in the same place twice. The road slices through the middle of the property and then circles behind it, ultimately joining itself and forming a loop for those brave enough to drive through the ruts and mud.

Main Street is reported to have more than 250 graves; however, only a fraction of these are marked. One of the main reasons is vandalism. Gravestones have been tipped over, broken, moved to other locations, and stolen. Many of the graves have also fallen off the eroding hillside. There are several large old trees that brood over the remaining stones as well as the charred remains of tree stumps that met an untimely end.

Satanism and the dark arts have played a substantial role in the unrest of this cemetery. While most of the nocturnal visitors are curious local teens, a dark factor has also been active there. It's not unusual to find tombstones defaced with pentagrams, skulls, demonic drawings, and black candle stubs. Inverted crosses have been scorched into the grass. Trees and shrubs have been set aflame, and the carcasses of small animals have been discovered draped over headstones and impaled on trees. An enormous gravestone from the 1900s sits perfectly in place. The sickening reality is that the entire stone is upside down. There were also rumors that Satanists unearthed decrepit caskets, pulled out the bodies, and used the remains in their rituals.

The stories surrounding Main Street Cemetery could fill an entire book. It has been attracting teenagers and curious ghost hunters for many years. Most residents of Hancock County have heard at least one horrifying tale about Main Street, and its reputation has been furthered along by its inclusion in several paranormal books. Details change over the years but the stories remain popular, especially among teenagers.

One account describes an old woman and her grown son. They allegedly lived in an outbuilding behind the cemetery, the remnants of an abandoned farm, in the late 1960s. The son was portrayed as mentally slow. There are different versions of this story, but the main one involves a group of teenagers who terrorized the couple. Their pranks and vandalism escalated, growing more and more violent, and tragically ended when they physically attacked the mother. When the son tried to help her, he was brutally murdered. His ghost reportedly roams the cemetery carrying a bow and arrow, hunting for teenagers who are causing trouble.

Another widely spread story is about a local man who shockingly discovered his wife was having an affair. Insane with rage and anger, he dragged her through the cemetery to a large tree. She kicked, screamed, and pleaded for her life, professing her innocence. Ignoring her cries, he formed a noose from a strong rope he had brought with him. He forced the noose roughly around her neck and pulled it tightly. As she struggled to breathe, he flung the other end of the rope over a thick tree branch and then yanked with all his might. Her nightgown-clad body was jerked into the air. After a macabre shudder, it finally went limp. Still seething with anger, the husband anchored the rope and left, only to return with a bow and arrow. Carefully aiming, he released the bowstring and pierced her lolling head with the arrow. Finally satisfied, he left her there, swinging from the tree in the moonlight. Her pale ghost is said to haunt the area surrounding her gruesome death, and her screams can still be heard echoing over the cornfields.

There are many stories involving children and babies. A disproportionate number of graves do appear to belong to children. One of these graves is rumored to belong to a child who was described as the devil's pawn. A tree in the shape of a pitchfork springs from the dirt above her body. If it is cut down or burned, it appears again the next day, unblemished and healthy. Many people claim to have heard the voices of children laughing and crying, and toys left in certain areas of the cemetery have inexplicably moved.

Keri and I have investigated Main Street/Hays Cemetery several times over the past few years, including once during the summer solstice, which garnered spectacular results. The first time we ventured up the foreboding dirt road was on a warm night in the spring of 2002. We were relatively new ghost hunters back then, and the only equipment we carried were a digital camera and a compass. We have returned many times since then, bringing newer and more sophisticated equipment. We have never left disappointed and have experienced many forms of paranormal phenomenon.

On a particularly active night, we concentrated our attention on the infamous tree where the scorned husband hanged his wife. The area surrounding it seemed charged with electrical energy, and the IR thermometer directed at the fork of the tree registered an astonishing temperature drop of twenty-two degrees. When I thrust my hand into this area, I got a painless but startling shock, as if from a faulty electrical wire. The hair on my arms and neck stood straight up. It almost crackled with energy. We also captured several large orbs in photographs of this area.

Not only were orbs captured by our digital cameras, they were also visible to the naked eye, a very unusual phenomenon. They appeared as gold or white globes and flitted through the tree branches, fading and brightening. At first, we believed them to be lightening bugs, but

Orbs that have been captured in photographs of Main Street Cemetery have also been seen by the naked eye. Photograph courtesy of Mary Ellen "Mellen" Hammack.

upon closer inspection found they were not. They floated in the air, some zipping erratically and some slowly bouncing. Occasionally they were joined by a small red orb. It was an awe-inspiring sight, and I could've spent hours standing there just watching them.

On other occasions, the cemetery was not as welcoming. We heard deep growls from the darkness, beyond the tree line; however, we never saw dogs in the area or heard barking. The guttural growls followed us as we walked along the trees, stealthily stalking our movements. It was quite frightening and something we have not experienced anywhere else. This particular phenomenon has happened several times to us and has been reported by many people over the past several years.

One night, I was walking slowly along the tree line, shining my flashlight on the ground and hoping not to trip on the many broken headstones. As I walked, I began to discern footsteps beside me, rustling through the dead leaves. I abruptly stopped, paused, and heard only silence. Assuming it was my imagination, I resumed walking, only to hear the steps again, mimicking my gait. I walked more quickly, and the footsteps shadowed me, getting increasingly louder. I slowed, and so did they. I shined my light into the trees, thinking perhaps some local teens were playing a joke on me, but nothing appeared in the flashlight beam but brush and tree trunks. Whatever walks the tree line of Main Street Cemetery has been haunting it for quite some time. Tales of this phenomenon have been shared since the early 1950s.

We have also heard the giggles of children during different visits. The laughter seems to come from near the family plot of the Eakins family. According to the stones, most of them died a few years after the Civil War. Whispers are often heard and recorded on EVP. The voices that we have captured have yet to be deciphered into words. Instead they sound like sighs or soft moans.

Even the most experienced ghost hunters are not immune to the phenomenon. One memorable evening came to an abrupt end when every member of our group suddenly bolted down Thomas Road, driven from the property by threatening growls and darting red lights that followed us through the darkness, not stopping until we had reached our cars. Some of the witnesses felt as if the lights were orbs, while others described them as glowing red eyes.

Main Street Cemetery has a long-standing and wide-spread notoriety, attracting ghost hunters and thrill seekers from Indiana and
beyond. Carol Mason, an avid ghost hunter, traveled from Grand
Rapids, Michigan, to experience the cemetery. She arrived about a
half an hour before sunset on a chilly day in November. "As soon as
I got out of the car, I could feel the activity. It immediately struck me
as just wrong. A feeling of sadness overwhelmed me, and I wanted to
get back in the car and drive away." Trying to shake off the feeling of
despair, Mason began exploring, taking some photographs and reading the headstones. "I felt like I wasn't welcome, like I had no business intruding there. As I went further into the cemetery, I noticed
mosquitoes buzzing around my head. This was really weird because
they don't come out that late in the year. I guess they didn't get that
memo because soon they were swarmed around me, and they were
hungry! They literally chased me down that dirt road and into my car.
I killed mosquitoes all the way back to Michigan."

Our EMF meters behaved erratically here although there is nothing to interfere with them. Because they refuse to stay at one level for
any amount of time, it's difficult to legitimately register their activity.
We had the same luck with a TriField natural EM meter. When left
alone in the middle of the area, it went off incessantly, the needle
moving continuously from one side to the other.

In the past couple of years, restoration efforts have greatly
improved the appearance of Hays Cemetery. It is well guarded by the
vigilant county sheriff's department, and those who trespass are
quickly ejected. The trees that formed the eerie canopy over Thomas
Road have been removed, and the rutted pathway has been graded
and paved with pristine white stones. The existing gravestones have
been repaired and scrubbed clean of graffiti, and the mysteriously
inverted stone has been righted back to its original position.
According to local gossip, a priest has blessed the area and exorcised
any evil entities. It now appears charming and quaint, nestled in the
soft and well-tended grass.

Did the loving attention heal this spot? Do those who rest there
finally slumber in peace? I recently visited Main Street on a lovely
spring afternoon, leisurely walking among the weathered old stones.
In spite of the near-perfect day, I still felt the sense of wrongness there.

I would like to believe that this cemetery has been released from the darkness that had gripped it for so long, but the back of my neck pricked with uneasiness. My camera, dangling from my wrist, suddenly flashed, and I couldn't remember turning it on. I quickly made my way back to the car, resisting the urge to break into a run and steadfastly ignoring the impulse to turn and look behind me. Unable and unwilling to explore any more, I hastily wheeled down Thomas Road, happy to leave Main Street and its many secrets safely behind me.

CHAPTER 9

Tuckaway House

(Lorri Sankowsky)

The soft sounds of jazz and gentle laughter filter through the swaying trees. The glow of candlelight sparkles in tiny window panes like diamonds, beckoning visitors. Chauffeurs in starched uniforms deposit vivacious men and women at the front walkway and swipe imaginary dirt from gleaming Duesenbergs. The gilded walls inside Tuckaway are as welcoming as the smiling butler answering the door. Enchanted party guests are enveloped warmly by the charm of the small but gracious home. Walt Disney is lounging at the dining-room table, doodling sketches of Mickey Mouse for Mary Pickford. Carole Lombard giggles beside him. Joan Crawford puffs from an ebony cigarette holder. Her eyes flash as she vehemently discusses the latest MGM studio gossip with Lionel Barrymore and Peter Lawford. Leslie Howard shyly requests a dance from Isadora Duncan, and they tango through the salon as Sergei Rachmaninoff plays the piano.

This scene is not far from reality in the little bungalow on North Pennsylvania Street. Aptly named Tuckaway, it is a home located in the heart of Indianapolis but feels miles away. Embraced by trees, insulated from the harsh urbanism surrounding it, Tuckaway is a golden jewel kept lustrous by its current owner, Ken Keene.

Tuckaway, built in 1906, began as an unremarkable cottage. It was constructed in a glen of trees on an ancient Indian burial ground. Clad in dull red-stained cedar clapboard, the home would have faded into obscurity if it had not captured the eye of Nellie and George Meier. Nellie looked beyond the plain exterior and saw potential in the little brown house. The couple purchased the home in 1910 and made several structural changes but never interfered with the trees that protected it so carefully.

George Phillip Meier was a renowned fashion designer, known not only in the United States but internationally as well. His dress designs were in high demand by the most fashionable and affluent women of the era. As a young man, George began his career as a tailor for men but his flair and sense of design were more suitable for women's wear. At one time, his shop occupied an entire floor of L. S. Ayres department store and employed several skilled seamstresses. His wedding-dress designs were particularly stunning. He was a dashing figure, perpetually well dressed, impeccably groomed, and graceful for a man over six feet tall. He had silver hair, wore a monocle, and had many distinguished and high-ranking friends. His dynamic personality and commanding presence might have overpowered a lesser woman, but his wife, Nellie, was up for the challenge.

Nellie Simmons Meier was a squat woman with a huge gift. As a young woman, she developed an interest in palm reading, mainly to set herself apart from the other girls who she felt were prettier and smarter than her. She became entranced and studied in earnest, practicing at church bazaars and charity events. Upon mastering the art, she found herself wildly popular and much sought after by both men and women.

She did not take her craft lightly. She studiously researched and collected data, meticulously recording her work and findings. Nellie did not tell fortunes. She considered palmistry a form of counseling and character analysis. She gave advice to her clients, helped them make decisions, and interpreted problems in their lives. Nellie's reputation grew, and several distinguished figures sought her advice, including Albert Einstein and James Whitcomb Riley.

Palmistry is an ancient art, traceable as far back as 3200 B.C., and is mentioned in the Old Testament of the Bible. Its popularity has waxed and waned, reaching high points in the Middle Ages and the Renaissance, dying out in the seventeenth century, and then surging again in the 1900s, along with the revival of spiritualism and paranormal studies. Some modern physicians, psychologists, and criminologists recognize that the unique lines and patterns of a person's palm directly correspond to their personality characteristics and that they can use this information accordingly.

It is often said that the future of our nation rests in the hands of our president. This was literally true during several years of Franklin Roosevelt's term in office, considering that Nellie Meier was reading his palm and advising him on decisions. Nellie read for Franklin and Eleanor Roosevelt several times, preserving their hand prints in black ink. When Mrs. Roosevelt visited Tuckaway for such readings, her Secret Service men would hide behind the large trees in the front yard so they would not draw unwanted attention. Nellie also visited the White House, where she read the hands of the president, his personal secretary, and several other associates and family members of FDR. Eventually, the palmistry sessions and character sketches began to alarm White House officials, who did not want the American public to know the influence that Nellie had on the first couple. They requested that Nellie refrain from publishing or even discussing the sessions, and Nellie readily agreed. After Nellie's death, Eleanor Roosevelt personally visited Tuckaway and removed all the palm prints and correspondence that pertained to her family. Many of them can be viewed at the Franklin D. Roosevelt American Heritage Center within the historic Union Station in Worcester, Massachusetts.

George and Nellie attracted a lively group of friends, and they loved nothing better than to entertain in their wonderful home. They became as well known for their soirées as they were for their respective careers. Weekends at Tuckaway were filled with laughter, music, and dancing. Nellie had a special floor installed in the salon to better enable guests to tango. The room also had superb acoustics, and many well-known pianists gave impromptu concerts there, including George Gershwin and Sergei Rachmaninoff. Her home was not large but, as current owner Ken Keene says, "It invoked a feeling of formality." Uniformed maids and butlers attended to guests. Exquisite foods were served from the best china, and guests wanted for nothing. An invitation to Tuckaway was treasured and a guarantee of a good time. People traveled for many miles to attend Nellie's parties, many from Hollywood. They were initially drawn by her palmistry skills and eventually charmed by her vibrant home.

As testament to Nellie's popularity, today the walls of Tuckaway are covered with autographed photos and handprints that she collected over the years. Famous faces from the twenties and thirties are frozen in time, haunting the hallways and rooms of Tuckaway as they once did in life.

Among them are Amelia Earhart, Ethel Barrymore, Walt Disney, Helen Hayes, Frederic March, Joan Crawford, and Carole Lombard.

Lombard, a sassy and beautiful actress, was happily married to Clark Gable. She was in Indianapolis to sell war bonds. Born in Fort Wayne, she wanted to assist the defense-bond campaign in her home state. Before she returned home, she made a visit to Tuckaway, drawn by Nellie's reputation. As Nellie peered into Lombard's palm, she was disturbed at what she saw. Alarmingly, she advised Lombard to be wary of impending danger and, above all, to not board a plane on her return trip. Nellie was deeply bothered by the outcome of the reading and further upset when Lombard smiled sweetly, thanked her, and left for the airport.

Lombard was not a woman easily swayed. Her mother, who had

The walls of Tuckaway House are covered with pictures of its illustrious former guests.

accompanied her on the trip, also had a bad premonition and begged Lombard to return via train. It was rumored that Lombard was anxious to return to Hollywood to keep an eye on Gable, who had recently started filming a movie with Lana Turner. Without hesitation, she boarded the TWA Skysleeper, along with her reluctant mother and twenty-one other people, mostly soldiers who were reporting for duty. The plane landed in Las Vegas, refueled, and was back in the air at 7:07 P.M. Thirty minutes later, it crashed into the side of Table Mountain, killing all those aboard. The cause of the crash remains a mystery. Eye witnesses report that the sky was clear and visibility was unlimited. The pilot had several years of experience and should've been well above the required altitude. The plane was new, and the engines and instruments had been checked shortly before take off.

Clark Gable, who had been awaiting the arrival of the plane in California, flew to the scene of the wreck immediately. A search party, lead by a Native American guide, forced its way up the snow-packed, rugged mountain, hoping for survivors. The impact of the crash had reduced the plane to rubble. The bodies of those aboard were recovered as much as possible. Lombard's left hand was never found, and Gable offered a reward for anyone who found her wedding ring. Today, a memorial plaque denotes the crash site. The plane engines, debris, and molten aluminum remain embedded in the mountainside. Determined fans continue to find relics in the area, including rivets, buttons, and even the metal closures of a bra.

Nellie and George continued to share Tuckaway with the cream of society. Eventually Nellie tired of her palmistry and threw her efforts into giving parties that were more and more fabulous. She wanted to be remembered as a gracious hostess and wanted all who entered her domain to feel loved and appreciated. She succeeded until the passing of her beloved George in 1932. Although she continued to go through the motions of life, her heart was heavy, and she eventually joined him, dying in 1944. Tuckaway was inherited by their niece, Ruth Cannon. Cannon had lived with the Meiers from the age of fifteen and was a trained dancer. She left her job as a dance teacher and returned to Indianapolis to live in and care for Tuckaway. For twenty-five years, Cannon maintained the home as best she could. Because of neglect and the general decline of the neighborhood, the home slowly began to deteriorate.

In 1972, Ken Keene was a young man looking for a fresh start. At the suggestion of his father, he began searching for a house in the dilapidated neighborhood of Meridian Park. The years had not been kind to the once fashionable area. The large homes that had originally been built by executives, politicians, and bankers were either vacant or in disrepair. They were, however, available at a very reasonable price. Keene vividly remembers the first time he saw Tuckaway. "I was on my lunch hour and went to see this house on the advice of a friend. At first, all I could see were leaves. I pushed my way through the overgrown shrubbery and trees and finally got a glimpse of the house underneath. I had this epiphany that I was home. It was so electric and powerful; I fell into a daze and didn't wake up until almost twelve hours later. I don't know what I had been doing for all that time."

Keene did know that he had to own this house. Everything clicked into place, and two weeks later, he purchased Tuckaway from Ruth Cannon for $12,500. Keene and Cannon became friends, and they spent long hours discussing the Meiers and their home. Unfortunately their time together was cut short by Cannon's death shortly afterwards.

The home was empty of furniture but was rich with personal notes, letters, documents, and books. These items included Nellie's numerous handprints and character analyses. They were found in the basement in soggy cardboard boxes intended for the trash. The items were rescued and cataloged, and a large portion of them were framed and displayed.

Keene began to restore the home, preserving instead of replacing. The interior walls, which were made of canvas, were restored to their original golden luster, and the unusual linoleum floor, manufactured in small limited editions by the U. S. Rubber Co., was cleaned and polished. Rather than try to re-create the exact furnishings that once decorated the home, he looked for authentic pieces that captured the spirit of the era. At times, he felt like an unseen force was guiding him to purchase various items. When put into place, the lamps, rugs, and other furnishings looked uncannily at home, as if they were meant to be there.

It was not long after Keene took possession of the house that strange things began to happen. Although he was alone, he heard voices in different parts of the house and the sounds of footsteps going up and down the stairs. Several times in the middle of the night, he was abruptly roused by the sounds of a raucous party going on in the salon. Furious, he would open his bedroom door, preparing to confront the intruders, and the sounds would stop.

Keene's bedroom is the room where George Meier died. The bed is tucked into a nook under a window, and the bed curtains that had originally draped George's bed are still in place. While sleeping in this bed one night, Keene opened his eyes and was stunned to see glowing green smoke floating directly above him. "It was awful! It hung in the air above me. Finally it morphed and flew up into the ventilation shaft." This experience happened about thirty years ago, a time when Keene was feeling overwhelmed and susceptible. During this time, his friends described him as possessed, and he had frequent bouts of sleepwalking. There was also a lot of paranormal activity happening. Eventually Keene made peace with the house and its ghostly inhabitants. Now he says that the ghosts of Tuckaway protect him and safeguard the house.

Occasionally Keene rented rooms to local college students. The room most commonly occupied was Nellie's bedroom, however no one seemed to be able to stay in that room for any period of time. Several young adults came and went over the years, most of them strangers to each other, yet their stories never changed. They told Keene that faces would appear in the ceiling as they were drifting off to sleep. They also heard whispers, and one poor girl reluctantly told Keene that her bedcovers had been ripped from the bed and swirled around the room. She convinced herself that it was a dream and willed her body to sleep. The next morning, she was terrified when she awoke and found her sheets and bedspread strewn all over the room. That was the last night she spent there.

One much repeated story took place on the old-fashioned sleeping porch. The porch had been added onto the second story and was surrounded with shutters that could be closed completely. The Meiers' guests called it the tree house, and it was a popular spot to escape the heat of the day or night. One evening, a friend of Keene's was hosting a *Great Gatsby* party at Tuckaway. All the guests were dressed in 1920s attire. As Keene carefully made his way through the crowded salon, balancing a tray of refreshments, he was approached by a timid young woman who was visiting for the first time. Harried and preoccupied,

Keene spoke to her briefly and told her to make herself at home. As he walked away, he turned over his shoulder and said, "Make sure to go see the sleeping porch upstairs!"

The girl nervously left the boisterous room and climbed the stairs as instructed. As she stepped out onto the sleeping porch, she saw another couple standing in the shadows. Embarrassed that she had interrupted what looked like an intimate encounter, she tried to shrink back into the hallway but it was too late. The couple turned toward her, and she saw that they were older and dressed for the theme of the party. The woman looked grandmotherly, and her short stature was accentuated by the very tall man at her side. He was at least six feet tall, maybe more. He had a silver moustache and a monocle in one eye. The couple smiled at the girl warmly, spurring her to approach them and introduce herself. As she drew closer, the elderly woman gave her a sassy wink and then they both faded and disappeared.

Keene laughs as he reminisces about what happened next. "We all heard an Alfred Hitchcock scream from upstairs. It just pierced the air. The piano player stops, everyone stops. We stood there staring as this poor girl runs down the stairs, throws open the door, and runs out into the street."

Her friend followed her, trying to calm her down and find out what had occurred. By this time, the curious party guests had all moved onto the porch, and they watched as the two girls had a heated discussion, accompanied with much arm flailing and furor. Shaking her head at the pleas to return to the party, the girl jumped in her car and sped off, never to return. When her friend told Keene the tale of what had happened on the sleeping porch, he knew that the couple could only have been Nellie and George.

Today Tuckaway is a little gem in the once again prestigious Meridian Park neighborhood. Keri and I agree that it's one of the most active places we have had the pleasure to investigate. Walking inside, I felt transported to another place and time. The house has an essence that is hard to describe. I would call it an air of anticipation and expectance, as if something enchanting is about to happen. I have been in many restored and historical homes and have loved something about all of them, but they have never taken over my senses as Tuckaway does. I feel different within its walls, more gracious, more congenial, and I feel welcome there, not just by Keene but by the house itself.

The house was certainly welcoming the night we did our investigation there. We were accompanied by well-known Indianapolis psychic Marilene Isaacs, who has been a guest at Tuckaway for several years. As we approached the front walk, the lights inside the home twinkled in the tiny panes of glass, like the mischievous twinkle in a child's eye. It looked delighted to see us.

We began with a tour through the home, led by the ever-charming Keene. His enthusiasm and love for the house radiated from him. Like the house, Keene loves to entertain and is most happy when Tuckaway is filled with guests. Before we left the salon, I set up a motion detector and pointed it into a corner directly in front of the piano. On the top of the piano, I placed a piece of equipment that our friend and fellow ghost hunter Chris Garrison made for us. It is called a voltmeter. Ghosts frequently draw on energy sources around them, successfully draining batteries in flashlights, cameras, and anything else they can use. The voltmeter was conceived as a way to scientifically prove battery drainage. It has a numbered dial and four fresh batteries. If the batteries begin to drain, the needle on the dial reflects it. We have used this piece of equipment often but have never had any substantial results. The position of the needle was noted both on paper and with our video camera.

Stepping away from the area, Keene began to tell us a little about the home's history, pausing here and there to point out certain photographs and handprints. We had barely gotten started when the motion detector on the piano unexpectedly chimed. Hurrying back to the salon, we found the room was empty. Glancing at the voltmeter, we were astonished to note that the needle indicated a substantial loss of battery power. To put it in perspective, we have left this device hooked up for several hours before and the needle had barely budged. Now it had moved almost an inch across the dial.

As our group moved from the salon into the hallway, we were deluged with paranormal occurrences that continued for much of the evening. The lights in the room dimmed and grew brighter. A cold spot moved about freely, approaching one person and then moving to the next one, as if we were being greeted by a hostess. We were able to track the progress of it, and it stayed near us most of the night.

A photograph of coauthor Lorri Sankowsky and psychic Marilene Isaacs shows them surrounded by orbs in Tuckaway House.

There were several areas in the house, the hallway in particular, that caused bouts of dizziness. As we began to make our way upstairs, Keene was speaking about the previous owner, Ruth Cannon, and how special he thought she was. He excused himself as the phone rang and stepped away to answer it. There was no one on the other end. We stopped to ponder this a moment when the delicious scent of perfume wafted down the staircase. Keene nonchalantly stated the scent was White Shoulders, Cannon's favorite. Noting our amazement at the two odd occurrences, Keene just shrugged and said, "It used to get under my skin a lot more than it does now."

During the time that George and Nellie occupied the house, they had noticed a few paranormal events. Or, rather, their dogs noticed them. Many times their dogs would run to an empty chair, look up, and wag their tails, as if waiting for a pat on their heads. This strange behavior occurred throughout the history of the house. Psychic Marilene Isaacs often felt the presence of several small pets.

A striking young man named Romeo unexpectedly arrived at the door while we were there. He was in town briefly and stopped by to visit Keene. Romeo had once rented a room in Tuckaway and shared this experience on the basement stairs. "I was walking up the stairs, and I felt a furry body brush by my leg. I stopped, knowing there was nothing there. As I stood there, I could hear the dog continue by me and on down the stairs, could even hear his claws tapping each step."

Continuing on with the tour, Keene showed us his bedroom where he had seen the mist floating over his bed and also the art deco black marble bathroom. Next, we walked out onto the sleeping porch, a delightfully cool and slightly secret place. Perched among the century-old trees, the porch feels isolated and, indeed, like a tree house, as it had been described by Nellie's guests. The sounds and smells of the surrounding city are filtered by the verdant leaves, and the traffic-clogged streets seem very distant.

We next visited the two guest bedrooms. As we walked into the larger bedroom, located in the front of the house, we were startled by the sudden clang of a Chinese gong, followed by a husky voice, introducing himself as Zultan, the fortune teller. Zultan was a motion-activated talking head, swathed in a turban and encased in an Oriental cabinet. He happily bellowed out prerecorded fortunes to those who walked by. After our initial shock, we listened to Zultan's spiel until Keene flipped off the switch, annoyed. "That thing goes off at all hours of the night, and here I am, jumping out of bed and certain that someone has broken in. Finally I pulled the plug from the wall, and guess what, it still goes off."

We briefly visited the remaining bedroom, which had belonged to Nellie. This was also the room where the renters had been driven away. It was charmingly petite and currently occupied by an antique mannequin who was wearing a beaded evening dress designed by George Meier. Keene told us that Nellie's furniture had been black lacquer, inlaid with mother-of-pearl and silver accents in true art deco style, and the furniture had been tiny to suit her diminutive height. We only stayed a moment, planning to spend more time there later in the evening.

Heading back down the hall, we had almost reached the stairs when the distinctive sound of the gong and the voice of Zultan began bawling out another fortune. Returning to the bedroom, we saw that the fortune teller's switch was still set to off. We left Zultan happily bobbing and prophesying in his case and went downstairs.

We toured the kitchen, dining room, garden, and finally Nellie's reading room. The reading room now served as a library where all her papers and hand prints were stored and displayed. It wasn't a typical library. Although papers and books were stacked on every available surface, the room felt like a quaint cottage, with floral prints, delicate art work, and of course, framed and autographed photos and handprints covering the walls. It was in this room where Nellie took her clients for palm readings, and we fully expected it to be one of the more active rooms. Contrary to our expectations, the room did not appear to have any paranormal energy at all. Isaacs felt that Nellie had grown tired of the room, having expended so much mental energy there that, in her older years, she almost dreaded entering it.

Only one unexplored area of the house remained—the basement. Basements tend to be scary places regardless of ghosts, and this one was no exception. We descended the stairs, almost shivering with anticipation. It was a typical basement—dark, creepy, and filled with unseen niches. One thing that did stand out was a huge rolled carpet that occupied a big chunk of floor space. Ken explained that a friend had sent it to him from the infamous Hollywood hotel the Chateau Marmont. A wooden table held one of Nellie's ouija boards, and more of her books were crammed onto shelves that lined the walls. A small storage room revealed a treasure trove of her personal belongings, strewn together in a cacophony of fabrics, beads, feathers, and sequins. Although the basement was interesting, we had no indication that spirits were present.

We decided to spend the majority of the evening in Nellie's bedroom. It felt even smaller as we piled in and made ourselves comfortable. Isaacs made herself comfortable in a tiny rocking chair next to the equally tiny fireplace. Settling into the chair, she said, "This room is literally vibrating with energy." As if in agreement, the EMF meter began to beep rapidly. We conversed quietly, discussing Nellie's life and the guests that had been entertained at Tuckaway. Keri remarked, "I wonder if George ever felt overshadowed by his wife's popularity?"

A moment later, a cold chill hit my back like an ice cube. I remained quiet, awaiting a reaction, and it wasn't long coming. Keri said that she was getting cold chills, too.

Considering that the spirits were being so communicative, we decided to try an experiment. Our EMF detector is a subjective tool. You can never be sure if it is reacting to physical energy or spiritual energy. Attempting to decipher between them, Keri asked whoever was present in the room to use the EMF meter as a way to communicate with us, simulating the yes and no response on a ouija board. The meter cheerfully beeped in agreement. "Is this George?" we asked. No response. "Is this Nellie?" No response. "Is this Ruth?" Nothing. The meter was stubbornly silent.

Isaacs mentioned a box of antique clothing that had recently been sent to Keene. The clothing had belonged to a child named Ruby, who would've been Keene's aunt but for her premature death. Ruby had died when she was twelve as a result of blood poisoning following a tonsillectomy. Keene had shown Isaacs a vintage sailor dress earlier in the evening and had left the box of clothes on the nightstand next to Nellie's bed. At the mention of Ruby's name, the EMF meter came to life, flashing and beeping rapidly. Keri moved the EMF meter closer to the box, and the beeping increased. Isaacs stated that it was definitely Ruby who was present in the room. "She likes this room. It is small like her, and she said it feels like a dollhouse. She is also very excited that we are here."

"Ruby, is that you?" The EMF responded so strongly that the red light, normally pulsating, remained lit. We asked Keene for more details about her, and he replied, "Ruby died in 1906 as a little girl. We have always held a place for her in our hearts but we didn't know a lot about her. This box of clothes is the only thing I have that belonged to her. And now it appears that she's become a spirit here." The EMF detector continued to respond.

Keene slumped into a melancholy mood and began wistfully discussing a close friend that he and Isaacs had shared named Michael. Michael died at a very young age, and his death affected Keene very deeply. As he discussed his friend, the EMF meter slowed and died. Isaacs remembered that she had last seen Michael at Tuckaway and commented on how much he had loved the house. Keene said, "Michael was an odd friend of mine. We weren't always that close but we were spiritually connected. He loved Tuckaway and always said he was inspired by it."

"Michael, are you here?" Again, the EMF meter began rapidly responding. Isaacs smiled and said she had hoped that Michael's spirit would visit them. Michael's presence was now added to the several entities that were already in the house. Nellie's tiny bedroom felt charged with energy, and I could almost feel them as they swirled around the room. Commenting on the cold chills became redundant.

We remained in the bedroom, awed by the EMF response and enjoying the electric energy that surrounded us. It is very rare to find a location that was so active, so exciting! Finally we began to feel drained and groggy. Although the beeps and flashes from the EMF showed no sign of slowing, we weren't as resilient and reluctantly agreed that it was time to say goodbye. We walked slowly down the stairs and into the salon where the lights flickered frantically, as if the spirits did not want us to depart. Upon gathering the equipment, we discovered that the voltmeter that had been left on the piano registered another significant amount of battery drainage.

Before we left, Keri asked Isaacs why so many spirits were drawn to Tuckaway. "It's because it is easy for them to be here. It's not so much the love of the house but the house itself is a portal. They can come and go easily. There is no separation of heaven and earth here. This is not so much a haunted place, but a timeless one."

Reflecting on Isaacs' words, we traversed the curving front path to the sidewalk. The reality of the urban setting jolted me back into the present. There were no chauffeurs, 1920s flappers sipping gin, or movie stars in sight. Just my car, waiting at the curb under a streetlight. I continued to feel disoriented on the drive home, as if I had just returned from a wonderful vacation and hadn't been ready to leave.

Tuckaway is more than just a house. It has a spirit and life of its own, unlike any other place that I have ever visited. Its walls are filled with history, its rooms charged with both the living and the dead. It will wrap you in its alluring atmosphere and draw you in, as it did to me. If you would like to experience Tuckaway for yourself, it is open for tours several times a year. It is also available for rent for parties and gatherings. Keene says that both he and the house come alive when a party is in full swing. "I don't feel this house is haunted," he says cheerfully. "I feel it's a spiritual place and that energy is always here."

CHAPTER 10

Indy's Nefarious Neighborhoods

(Lorri Sankowsky)

Home is where the heart is but it's also where the haunts are. Like it or not, many homeowners find themselves cohabitating with uninvited and unwelcome spirits. There are areas in Indianapolis that have higher levels of ghostly activity than normal, and not all of them are aging, historical neighborhoods. Ghosts do not care if a house is a year old or a hundred years old. It's easy to imagine ghosts winsomely winding through the restored streets of Lockerbie Square or the Old Northside. It's harder to imagine them lingering in a newly constructed, entirely modern condominium or vanishing in and out of the walls of a multimillion-dollar home on Geist Reservoir. It does happen though—a lot.

Keri and I have investigated homes in almost every corner of the city. The people who contact us aren't looking for publicity. They are looking for answers. Because of privacy issues, a few of the really interesting houses that we have investigated must remain confidential. Most homeowners do not want their house labeled as "haunted." They might be surprised to learn that they are not the only house on the block that is having paranormal problems.

GEIST RESERVOIR

One of the most affluent sections in Indianapolis is the area surrounding Geist Reservoir. The shores of Geist are crowded with exclusive, multimillion-dollar homes, occupied by prominent and powerful people. Professional athletes, politicians, local media personalities, renowned doctors, and Governor Mitch Daniels own homes on or near the thirty-five-mile long shoreline. The reservoir is the second largest lake in Indiana, spanning three counties and four zip codes. Although it covers a lot of area, the water seldom reaches a depth of more than ten feet. Fall Creek flows into the northeast corner and resumes again on the other side of the dam, located on the southern tip.

The history of Geist Reservoir is a troubled one. Shady deals, bribery, and even murder are rumored to have occurred during its inception. The reservoir was developed in the late 1940s by the Indianapolis Water Co. to ensure a plentiful supply of water for the city. Its namesake, Clarence Geist, was a free-wheeling tycoon who bought the water company in 1912. At one time, he owned more than one hundred utility companies worth fifty-four million dollars. Geist also owned several exclusive country clubs and used them to his full advantage, enjoying the privilege and prestige that his money bought him. He was known for spending his money wildly and freely yet seldom on charitable causes, which explains why his legacy is not well known.

Soon after his purchase of the water company, Geist found himself embroiled in controversy. A mysterious illness began afflicting local citizens. The cause was eventually traced to the drinking water. Because its normal dumping grounds were closed for repairs, Citizens Gas Co. had been dumping its contaminants into Fall Creek. The gas company stated that the city of Indianapolis had instructed them to do so. The city denied this and blamed the water company. Both the water company and the city blamed Citizens Gas. Fingers were pointed and accusations were made, but a resolution was never reached.

The next upheaval began in 1913, when plans to develop Geist Reservoir began in earnest. Clarence Geist was advised that the current water supply would not be sufficient to meet the needs of the rapidly growing city. Not one to tarry, Geist spent the 1920s and '30s purchasing acres of land in the Fall Creek Valley to make room for the reservoir he envisioned, ignoring the pleas of citizens who feared sharp rate hikes and were already reeling from the Great Depression. Most of the acreage was obtained easily, preying on cash-strapped farmers, however there was a major roadblock to his plan. This obstacle was a tiny hamlet named Germantown.

Germantown was located near what is now the Bridgewater neighborhood. It was established in 1834 as the result of a murder. An

Algonquin Indian was murdered in the nearby town of Oaklandon. The German immigrants were so disturbed by the incident that they formed their own community on the northern banks of Fall Creek. The main street of Germantown is now the entrance road to the Geist Sailing Club.

Life was good in the ill-fated town. Residents were content with their diminutive community. There was a general store, post office, shoemaker, furniture factory, church, and grist mill surrounded by small farms. There were also a handful of larger estates, consisting of vast barns, several outbuildings, miles of wooden fences, and nice homes.

The citizens of Germantown were outraged as the water company took over their town, buying what land they could and forcefully taking land from those who resisted. They had no recourse against the water company, and soon their sleepy little town was deconstructed, acre by acre. Helplessly they stood back and watched as the redirected water flooded the valley and engulfed life as they knew it.

All that remains of Germantown now rests beneath the murky depths of Geist Reservoir. Virtually forgotten, the town occasionally makes its presence known. Fishermen on the reservoir often tell tales of snagging their fishing lines and anchors on the old timbers. Experienced boaters stay far away from the submerged main street, fearful the old structures might damage their boats. During times of drought, the church steeple protrudes above the waterline as an eerie reminder of what lies below.

The ill will towards the reservoir continued through the years. Swimming, boating, and fishing were banned, angering those who could only enjoy the beauty of the lake from the shore. No development along the shoreline was allowed, and conservationists who pushed to establish a public park were disappointed when they couldn't afford the price the water company demanded.

The 1960s finally brought some changes, although rumors of shady deals, bribery, and bitter disagreements continued. Development slowly encroached, beginning with a public observation area near the dam and a small public boat ramp. The following years brought more and more development. Today, the area is saturated with luxurious homes, exclusive restaurants, and a general air of affluence, a suitable tribute to Clarence Geist.

The glamorous life in the upscale neighborhoods of Geist Reservoir is not always as care free as you might imagine. Certain areas have high incidents of paranormal phenomenon. Well-known psychic Marilene Isaacs specializes in spiritually cleansing homes. She gets more requests from the Geist area than any other area in Indianapolis. She believes that all hauntings stem from the ground and what has taken place there. When the ground is disturbed, the spirits become disturbed also. Artificially flooding what was once a fruitful area filled with wildlife would be disturbing enough, but what if graves and burial grounds were also affected?

There are no official burial records but it's likely that the vast area of Geist Reservoir covers at least a few pioneer and Native American burial plots. Water is also a well-known conductor for spirits and energy. The disturbed energy combined with the excellent conduit of the reservoir is almost a guarantee that paranormal activity occurs in a large percentage of adjacent homes.

Tempting as it is, we cannot divulge any details regarding our private investigations in Geist. Rumors of ghosts could deflate property values by thousands of dollars. The troubled homeowners who have contacted us are highly regarded professionals in their fields, not the sort of people who would openly discuss items levitating in their libraries or whispers heard in their state-of-the-art home theaters. As a final, ironic tribute, the word "Geist" is German for "ghost." Maybe the former Germantown citizens are having the last laugh.

BRIDGEPORT

Performing in-home investigations can be either an exciting experience or the dullest evening imaginable. Occasionally, no matter how much activity a home normally has, the hours spent there will not be fruitful. Keri and I have spent eons sitting in cramped, dark rooms waiting on apparitions that never appear. It is frustrating to both the investigator and the homeowner. The homeowner is more likely to get upset, unable to understand why their gregarious ghosts choose this particular time to remain quiet. It's rare for an investigator to experience activity at the level the homeowner has been encountering. Keeping this in mind, consider the chances of experiencing two phenomenally active homes located within sight of each other.

The Bridgeport area is on the far west side of Indianapolis in Wayne Township. It began as an unremarkable railroad town and faded into obscurity, leaving only its name. It now consists of clusters of housing additions such as Countryside, Salem Creek, Berkshire, Bridgeport Commons, and Spring Valley. Nothing in this pleasant suburbia would lead anyone to suspect the turbulent activities that have been experienced by two unrelated households, but something is definitely amiss in this land of soccer moms and minivans.

We were first contacted by the Johnson family in October 2002. For privacy reasons, their name and identifying details have been changed. The Johnsons seemed like a normal family and were very hesitant about asking for our help. Mrs. Johnson, in particular, was at her wits end. At her request, we visited their home for a preliminary investigation.

We joined the Johnsons and their two children around the dining-room table. Slowly they began to explain what had been happing in their home. They inundated us with stories of sights, smells, and sounds that they had experienced, describing shadow figures, electrical problems, odd odors, footsteps running down their hallway, doors opening and closing, furniture moving, and an episode of hair pulling.

The children were having lurid dreams of statues that suddenly opened their eyes and stared at them. Floating figures appeared in their bedrooms, hovering above their beds. One child described a family of ghosts that she frequently saw in the backyard. The spectral family didn't trouble her, however a new spirit had recently joined them. Her cherubic face was disturbingly serious as she described it. "It looks different than the rest of them. Darker, blacker, and it never smiles."

Mrs. Johnson had been doing some initial investigations of her own and shared with us a video tape she had taken of orbs moving about her living room. She also shared a compelling story involving a large dry-erase board. One morning she awoke to discover three stick figures drawn on the board. At first she suspected the children and was angered that they were roaming through the house at night. That conclusion was proven wrong when she realized the figures were drawn at the top of the board. Even if they had stood on chairs, the children could not have reached that high up. Puzzled but not yet fully awake, she erased the board and left the playroom to start a pot of coffee. Several moments later, she walked by the playroom again and glanced inside. What she saw made her jump, slinging the coffee through the air. She could only stand in mute horror, watching as the spattered coffee slowly dripped down the shiny white board. The three stick figures had miraculously reappeared, exactly where they had been before.

We made plans to return to the house for a full investigation and advised Mrs. Johnson to keep a written journal of occurrences, noting the time, place, and any other information to determine if there was a pattern. Driving home, I decided to play the audio tape that had been recorded during the interview. The car was warm and quiet as I listened to the voices of the Johnson family and empathized with the fear and dread they were experiencing. A few minutes into the recording, I was startled by a cacophony of whispers. It was as if several people had been in the next room during the interview. They were furiously discussing our conversation. I listened intently, rewinding and playing back portions. Their exchange ebbed and waned, mirroring the live conversation that was taking place at the dining-room table. It was difficult to make out their exact words but one part of the tape was clear. As Mrs. Johnson discussed the orbs on her video tape, the whispering voice hissed, "Orb? What's an orb?" This was followed by excited and incensed murmuring.

We returned to the Johnson home a few weeks later for a full investigation. We asked that the children not be present and that all electrical power to the home be turned off. During the several hours that we spent there, we witnessed a multitude of unexplained occurrences. Sounds emanated from different areas of the home. Metal clothes hangers clanged together in a bedroom closet, and glass tinged as if someone were giving a champagne toast. Faint voices could be heard in the kitchen.

Orbs were photographed with the digital camera so often that they became redundant. An interesting quasar type of shape appeared in the view finder of the night-shot video camera, visible for several minutes. It began as a round orb, elongated to a pencil shape, and then expanded in the middle to form a cross. It also seemed to respond to us, changing shape quickly when we were attentive to it and then slowing if our attention was diverted elsewhere.

The family dog, which had been relegated to the garage, had been very well behaved. Suddenly it began to inexplicably howl and frantically bark. Mrs. Johnson rushed to the door and let the dog inside. It immediately urinated on the kitchen floor. The normally friendly dog spent the remainder of the night cowering under the kitchen table.

Although the main power source had been shut off, electromagnetic activity was detected in every room with the handheld meters. The TriField natural EM meter was left in the kitchen, where it sporadically went off over and over again. Adjustments were made to fine-tune the sensitivity, but it still registered some form of energy.

Mrs. Johnson was relieved that we also experienced the disturbances that had been plaguing her family. She pleaded with us to find out more information on whom or what was haunting her home. We decided to have a psychic walk through and see if he could pick up any clues. Psychics can be invaluable during investigations such as this one. Their sixth sense is able to supply missing information that scientific gadgets simply cannot.

The psychic reported that there were six entities in the home. Only one of them was capable of creating the disturbances that had been witnessed. This spirit had been dormant but recent events had provoked it. In an attempt to protect the children, it had been trying to frighten the parents. The psychic reported that the spirit's sense of responsibility and love for the children permeated the house. It had been trying to change the behavior in the home via poltergeist activity.

A view out the Johnsons' back door would reveal the site of another highly active home in the Bridgeport area. In 1997, Marilyn Smith (name changed for privacy) contacted the Indiana Ghost Trackers to request an in-home investigation. Smith was no stranger to paranormal activity. She kept detailed records of the occurrences in her home for several years, noting date, time of day, and activity, hoping to one day find an explanation or at least a pattern.

Smith spent her preteen years in an older home not far from where she presently lives. The paranormal activity that has always surrounded her began there. Her father had passed away suddenly, leaving her mother with little money. Distraught, her mother dragged her bewildered children from bed and left in the middle of the night to find a more economical place for them to live. She settled on an innocuous farmhouse because of its roominess and affordability. It still stands today, the burgeoning town of Avon growing up all around it.

From the very beginning, Smith hated the house. She would spend many hours playing in a nearby cemetery, staying outdoors as long as she could before returning to the stressful atmosphere of her new home. It was in the house that she first experienced threatening and malevolent spirit activity.

Unexplainable events began to happen. Heavy footsteps were heard running up and down the basement stairs. Sounds of glass crashing to the floor in the basement became common. Family photos, framed and hanging on the wall, lifted themselves up and off of their nails and flew across the room. Ashtrays full of cigarette butts and ashes would suddenly fly into the air and overturn, scattering their contents on the floor. As Smith watched, a key in the bathroom door turned of its own accord, and the door was slowly pulled open. The occurrences were witnessed by the entire family as well as visitors, however, the Smith family had nowhere to go to escape. They were barely making the rent and felt trapped in the isolated house. Smith wistfully describes her impressions of the house, "It was just evil. There is no other word for it. I was afraid every moment that I spent there. My mom couldn't accept what was happening around us, so eventually she would just dismiss it. Finally me and my brother just stopped talking about it, too. What else could we do?"

In 1995, a newly married Smith settled into a home in the Countryside neighborhood with her husband and infant son. She loved the area, loved her new home, and happily went about creating a stable and happy life with her family. The paranormal activity that had haunted her teenage nights had long been forgotten.

In January 1997, Smith's sense of peace was shattered by an incident that occurred in her kitchen. Her toddler son was safely behind his baby gate, playing in the playroom. She pulled a full trash bag out of the trash bin, set it on the kitchen floor and tied the top into a knot. She stepped back a few feet to visually check on her son and then turned to the kitchen counter to make a shopping list. A wooden chair, which normally rested under the dining table several feet away, was inexplicable sitting next to the bag of trash. Smith froze and called to her son, who answered her from the other room. No one else was present in the home. Nervously chuckling, she carried the chair back to its original spot and walked into the bathroom. She was only gone for a few seconds. When she returned to the kitchen, the chair had not only been moved from the dining room into the kitchen, but it had also been lifted, set on top of the bag of trash, and was now leaning against the dishwasher.

Smith hastily grabbed her son and flew out the house, only to realize that she had nowhere to go. The memory of the constant fear she had felt in the farmhouse began to overwhelm her. After several tearful hours, she decided that she would not let fear rule her life again and vowed to learn what she could about the paranormal in hopes that she could understand and tolerate what was happening. She became a voracious reader, devouring stacks of books on ghosts, haunted houses, and ghost hunting. The Internet unlocked even more information. She began documenting the events in her home, keeping detailed records of each event.

Over the years, a family of what she refers to as shadow people have been sighted. The family consists of a father, a mother, a small boy, and a cat. Her two sons refer to the family as their guardian angels and see them frequently. The shadow family reacts to the children and also with each other. One night her older son was lying in bed awake and heard the shadow boy playing with his toys. The shadow mother appeared to scold the boy, saying, "You are making too much noise, and you're going to wake him up!" The shadow boy reluctantly put down the toys and followed his mother, dissipating through the closet door.

More disturbing than the innocuous shadow family is the frequent appearance of doppelgängers. "Doppelgänger" is German for "doublewalker," a shadow self that is believed to accompany everyone, sometimes referred to as an evil twin. It is also described as the ghost of a living person. Usually they are portrayed as mischievous and malicious. Doppelgängers have been seen throughout history, and seeing one is commonly thought of as a harbinger of death or misfortune. It is said that Queen Elizabeth I of England was shocked to see her doppelgänger laid out on her bed. She died shortly thereafter. Percy Bysshe Shelly, a great poet, encountered his doppelgänger in Italy. It silently pointed toward the Mediterranean Sea. Not long after, Shelley was in a sailing accident and drowned in the very spot the phantom had indicated.

Smith does not think that the doppelgängers in her home are harmful. To the contrary, she believes they are spirits who are trying not to frighten her by appearing as loved ones. They normally appear to her as images of her own children. In one instance, she awoke in the early morning to see her youngest son running down the hallway with his beloved pacifier in his mouth. She scrambled out of bed, calling out to him that it was too early to wake up. She followed him down the hallway, only to find an empty room. Walking back down the same hallway, she discovered him asleep in his bed. A few months later, she was sitting on her older son's bed, reading him a bedtime story, when he looked up and said, "Hi, Daddy!" Smith left his room, thinking her husband was home from work early. Not finding him, she phoned his workplace, several miles away, and he answered. As recently as July 2007, Smith witnessed her younger son run across the kitchen and dissipate into the refrigerator door.

The helpful ghost of Smith's own father, who died in 1970, also visits the home. During breakfast one morning, her son told her about seeing Grandpa in the bathroom. He described him perfectly, although there aren't any photos of him displayed. He reported that Grandpa told him, "Shhhh! I am just here to fix the leak." Smith left her sons at the dining table to finish their cereal and went to the bathroom to investigate. Sure enough, a minor but long-term leak in the base of the toilet had miraculously been fixed and remains dry to this day.

Although investigators from the Indiana Ghost Trackers as well as a handful of psychics have been to her home, Smith resisted having a full-blown investigation conducted and has not learned the identity of the ghosts. She has stopped most of her own investigation but is still tempted to take digital pictures from time to time. She was quite successful at recording EVP but has ceased recording as well, saying it was "too creepy." She remains very active in paranormal investigation and has developed an interest in other haunted locations, just not the one in which she lives. She now coexists with her multitude of shadow people and ghosts, imploring them not to scare the babysitter when she leaves and scolding them when they scare her friends and relatives. She doesn't know why they have chosen her

Although a full investigation has not been conducted, a home in the Bridgeport neighborhood revealed paranormal activity, including orbs. Photograph courtesy of Mary Ellen "Mellen" Hammack.

house, or herself, but she speaks kindly of them, describing how turmoil in the household seems to stir up their activity. "When we are stressed, they get stressed. Whenever there is arguing, big decisions to be made, or even medical issues, they let us know that we are not alone. They care about us."

Smith is not afraid of her home, or her ghosts, but she still maintains a fear of the old white farmhouse from her childhood, an atmosphere completely different from the one she lives in now. At our urging, she agreed to take us to the home but refused to get out of the car. The farmhouse has not changed, but now instead of being isolated in fields of corn, it is surrounded by new homes that accentuate its shabbiness. A new unsuspecting family resides within. As we sat in Smith's car, quietly observing the house and wondering if its ghostly inhabitants were still there, I withdrew my tape recorder and pressed record.

Smith told us more details. After her family moved from the home, her best friend and her parents moved in. They were also looking for an affordable house with enough bedrooms for their children. Smith's friend experienced the same kind of poltergeistlike activity— the sound of footsteps, glass breaking, objects being moved and sometimes being thrown. Her friend was under a lot of personal stress as well and ultimately tried to commit suicide while she lived there. Remarkably, after her friend and her family moved out, Smith's brother and his family moved in. She questioned his judgment, asking him if he remembered what had happened there when they were kids. He laughed and recalled that it was just their imagination, that nothing would happen to either him, his wife, or his young daughter. It wasn't long after that when Smith's niece told her a terrifying tale. She said that every night a little green man with red eyes would come to visit her in her bed. Smith tried to hide her overwhelming fear and playfully asked the little girl what the man's name was. The answer chilled her to the bone. With childhood innocence, the two-year-old replied, "His name is Dobby Dobb."

"Dobby Dobb" is an ancient reference to an imp of Satan, an evil goblin who does the work of the devil. In the United Kingdom, he was so feared that villagers hung holed stones, known as dobby stones, over their doorways to prevent him from entering.

A few days later, I sat down to transcribe the tape of Smith's interview. I retreated to the only quiet place in my home, my bedroom, and made myself cozy under the warm comforter with a pad of legal paper and my tape recorder. The tape was several hours long, and writer's cramp was setting in toward the end of it. My eyelids were getting heavy as I listened to our conversation as we sat outside the farmhouse. My finger was moving to the stop button when I was startled by a sound that I couldn't identify. I sat up straight and rewound a portion of the tape, listening closely. As Smith pointed to the bedroom window, indicating where her niece's bedroom had been, a deep male voice could be heard on the tape. It was not a whisper, and the words were not slurred. It was very clear and deliberate, and my heart still pounds whenever I hear it. Recorded inside the car in a male voice were the words "Dobby Dobb."

IRVINGTON

The Irvington neighborhood is on the east side of Indianapolis and straddles Washington Street, originally known as the National Road. The scholarly founders of the area thought the curving brick-lined streets and brooding Victorian homes were eerily similar to the town featured in the literary horror classic *The Legend of Sleepy Hollow* by Washington Irving and named it accordingly. A concrete bust of Irving was also erected as an homage. The streets were intentionally planned too narrow and curvy for carriage operators, thereby protecting the towering Victorian homes from curious gawkers. In 1875, Butler University was founded by abolitionist Ovid Butler. By World War I, more than one thousand students were in attendance. Irvington's growth was also boosted by railroad and streetcar access.

In spite of its grandiose beginnings, Irvington began to decline in the mid-1900s as city dwellers began a mass exodus for the suburbs. The university moved to its present location in the Butler Tarkington neighborhood. The once bustling rail depot was closed, and the streetcars became defunct. Many homes fell into disrepair, their aging owners too plagued with health problems to maintain them. Several of the larger homes were divided into apartments. The once beautiful circles and fountains became weed choked and forlorn, and eventually Irvington became a place to avoid after nightfall.

Like the Headless Horseman relentlessly riding through the hills of Sleepy Hollow, the stubborn neighborhood of Irvington refused to give up. A small but vocal group of homeowners fought to protect and restore their beloved streets and were soon joined by young couples, lured by the affordability of the grand homes and not deterred by the obvious work they required. Their ranks swelled, and today the Irvington neighborhood is buoyed with many active committees such as its Community Council, Garden Club, and Historical Society. Once again the streets of Irvington are alive and occupied by those who adore it.

The lively homeowners are not the only spirits creating a ruckus in this charming area. Irvington can also boast of more ghosts per square mile than any place in Indianapolis. Irvington has long been fond of ghost stories and all things spooky. Its annual Halloween Festival draws thousands of spectators every year and culminates with a walking ghost tour. Residents and shopkeepers revel in talking about their ghosts and consider them just another added bonus in their already bountiful neighborhood.

The commercial district in Irvington consists of several glass-front shops facing each other along Washington Street. There are two restaurants along this main thoroughfare, and both are said to be haunted. Dufours Restaurant occupies a portion of a building that previously was home to Haag's Drug Store. In 1933, the drug store was the site of a botched robbery attempt by infamous bank robber John Dillinger. Those who dine at Dufours may experience the presence of a helpful ghost, probably not Dillinger, who reminds employees to lock the front door. The Legend Restaurant is located a few storefronts down and has also experienced unexplainable noises, such as chairs being moved in the dining room while the restaurant is closed.

Jeff Coppinger, the owner of Lazy Daze Coffeehouse, has had his share of strange events. "I'm a skeptic, you know" he says. "But these things happened, and I can't explain them." Coppinger, who bought the coffee shop about three years ago, goes on. "It was about a month after I bought it. The shop was closed, and I was there working on the computer. It was a cold, dreary, quiet day." Coppinger laughed. "The kinda day a ghost would like. Anyway, all of a sudden I got a cold chill, and something whispered, 'Who are you?' I turned around but no one was there. The door was locked, and I was the only one in the building! After that, nothing happened for a while, and then one morning I was opening up. I always used to set up a chess set for people to play. I set out all the chess pieces and had turned around to fluff up the couch. When I turned back around, all the chess pieces were in place except they had all moved up one row. I asked the guy who was working with me if he had messed with it, but he hadn't been near it. It was pretty freaky!" Coppinger also said that he occasionally sees shadowy figures moving in the hallway. He remains skeptical but says, "Hey, this is Irvington. They say there are lots of ghosts here."

A restaurant of a different sort, For The Love of Dogs, A Dog Bakery, opened a location in Irvington in May 2005 and recently added a pet boutique. The staff there have experienced a few different kinds of phenomenon. "Lights flicker, and the TV changes channels," explains founder Christopher Hill. "One morning we came in and all the dog food bags had been taken off the racks in the middle of the store and stacked neatly in a corner. I tried to blame it on my partner, but he reminded me that I was the one who had closed the night before."

The Irvington Masonic Lodge had the unfortunate luck to be

designated Lodge Number 666, the "Number of the Beast" and long associated with Satanism. It is a looming art deco building, filled with carved woodwork and marble. In accordance with the Masonic tradition, the triangle and the number three are prevalent everywhere. Freemasonry is the largest and the oldest worldwide secret organization. Although based on a morale code, Freemasonry is not a religion itself. It's an organization based on secrets, rituals, and mysticism whose members remain tight lipped. Irvington Masonic Lodge was rumored to have hosted secret meetings of the Ku Klux Klan during the 1920s. The rumors make sense, considering that the grand dragon of the Indiana Ku Klux Klan, David Curtis Stephenson, lived a couple blocks away.

Dark secrets and mystical powers weren't enough to scare off current owner, Thom Zimmerman, who gladly purchased the defunct but still beautiful building in the late 1990s. During restoration, workers were spooked by shadowy shapes that glided from one room to another and heavy wooden doors that suddenly slammed shut. They also reported sudden drops in temperature and odd electrical quirks. A few of them were tapped on the shoulder while they were working, only to turn and find themselves in an empty room. Nothing this dramatic occurred during our investigation of the building other than some orbs appearing in photos.

A picturesque highlight of the Irvington neighborhood is South Irving Circle. The circle is at the intersection of Audubon Street and University Avenue. In the middle is a brick fountain lined with park benches and also the bust of Washington Irving. The circle, officially the smallest park in Indianapolis, is a popular gathering spot and often the site of summer concerts, poetry readings, and other cultural events. This area is so beloved that it has an entire committee of people, known as the Friends of Irving Circle, who devote their time and effort to maintain and beautify it. The circle also has its share of ghosts. A young woman, dressed in white and crying into a lace handkerchief, has often been seen walking from one side of the circle to the other. Another spirit, this one an elderly man sporting a beard and dressed in period clothing, has caused more than a little distress by suddenly appearing in the middle of Audubon Avenue and startling oncoming motorists. The fountain has been the unintended

148 ❦ GHOST HUNTER'S GUIDE TO INDIANAPOLIS

target of swerving cars more than once, and drivers often blame an older gentleman who appears out of nowhere.

Trains have not visited Irvington since the early 1900s but it's hard to convince local homeowners. Once a bustling and exciting stop, the railway depot is now long gone. The weed-clogged tracks are still visible in some areas, though, and standing on the rails, it's easy to imagine the snort of the steel horse charging through the trees, billowing black smoke and orange sparks. This railway is also the sight of the largest mass ghost sighting in the United States. The phenomenon is known as the Lincoln Ghost Train, and it has been seen and heard by hundreds of people for more than 140 years.

President Abraham Lincoln was known for his belief in the paranormal. He frequently held séances in the White House, and it's said that he had a premonition of his own death. His ghost has been seen roaming the White House by several people, including Eleanor Roosevelt, who allegedly befriended the melancholy spirit. After his assassination, Lincoln's body was transported on a special train to Illinois for burial. The train was bedecked with black mourning cloth, and a portrait of the president was attached to the cowcatcher in front. His coffin rode in a special car and was raised so that mourners could see it pass by. The train slowly wound through towns and farm land as citizens kneeled on the edges of the tracks, mourning their dead president. As the black train inched by, clocks stopped ticking and dogs howled uncontrollably. It was estimated that one-third of America's population witnessed the grievous procession.

The immense outpouring of grief left an indelible mark along Lincoln's route, and every spring, the Lincoln Ghost Train once again repeats the long journey. Those who have seen it say that it is manned by a crew of skeletons, dressed in Union blue. The first car is occupied by a glowing orchestra of skeletons, including a violinist, flutist, and drummer, all being led by a skeletal conductor. Their funeral dirge is barely audible but unmistakable. The last car holds the crepe-draped coffin and is accompanied by swirling blue wisps thought to be more spiritual soldiers paying their respects.

Many witnesses have not actually seen the train but have heard its whistle blow and smelled the smoke from its stack. During its procession, railroad crossing gates inexplicably lowered and remain down for as long as it takes for the phantom train to pass. An unearthly blue glow radiating from the rails, followed by a blanket of icy darkness, is an indication that the train is about to make an appearance. Those brave enough to remain by the tracks experience the ground shaking and a huge gust of floral-scented air.

Irvington residents have come to expect the Lincoln Ghost Train as matter of factly as they accept all their ghosts. Every April, lights dim and clocks stop, startling newcomers and amusing long-time residents who just shrug and say, "Must be spring. There's the ghost train!"

Several prominent homes in Irvington are also inhabited by spiritual specters. Considering the haunted trains, streets, and businesses, I would be disappointed if ghosts hadn't made their way into the stately Victorian homes. The Applegate House stands on the western edge of Irvington, near the original location of Butler University. Former residents often remarked about a smoky black figure in the shape of a young boy and a closet that remained so cold that frost would appear on the inside of it in the middle of summer.

Another haunted home is the antebellum mansion once owned by the grand dragon of the Indiana Ku Klux Klan, David Curtis Stephenson. Stephenson was a rich, hedonistic, and very powerful man with a bad temper. He considered himself above the law and was used to getting what he wanted. In 1925, Stephenson wanted a pretty young government worker named Madge Oberholtzer, who just happened to live a few blocks away in her parents' home. Oberholtzer rebuffed his advances, and Stephenson became more and more obsessed with her. Naïve and unsuspecting, Oberholtzer responded to a summons from Stephenson to take some late-night emergency dictation. She arrived at the mansion to find him drunk and belligerent and finally accepted the drink he offered her, intending to make her escape soon after.

The drug that he had secretly added to her drink took affect quickly, and Oberholtzer's limp body was transported to the train station and deposited in a private car. Over the next several days, Stephenson brutally assaulted and tortured her until she became so weak and sick that she was immobile. Stephenson returned to Irvington, confining Oberholtzer in a room above the carriage house. Her condition worsened, and Stephenson finally became nervous. He ordered one of his bodyguards to secretly return her to her parents' home, planning to deny any involvement, however the clumsy bodyguard was spotted as he was leaving Oberholtzer's bedroom.

Her parents found her on the bed writhing in agony. A physician was summoned and became physically ill at the extent of her injuries. In addition to internal injuries, her body was covered with bruises and cuts, including human bite marks. One of the bites had become so infected that she eventually contracted blood poisoning. Oberholtzer fought for her life for almost a month. She was able to give a statement to her lawyer, naming Stephenson and revealing what he had done to her. Her story soon made national news, and crowds gathered in front of her home, awaiting her death knell. Stephenson was eventually arrested and charged for her murder, successfully ending his reign as a powerful leader and also irretrievably damaging the existence of the KKK in Indiana. He served a thirty-one year prison term and left the state upon his release, still vehemently denying any involvement in the crime.

The Stephenson Mansion stood empty for many years, but sounds of a loud party would often drift across the lawn. Although electricity remained shut off, lights would appear in the windows, going on and off as if someone were walking through the rooms. The smell of cigar smoke was a common occurrence as well. Madge Oberholtzer's home is also paranormally active. During stormy nights, Oberholtzer is said to been seen peering out her bedroom window whenever lightening streaks across the sky. Some people report seeing her as she was after her death, blindingly pale with flowers draped over her crossed arms.

The beautiful red-brick Julian Mansion was constructed by George Julian, an Indiana congressman, in the late 1800s. He retired to Irvington with his beloved wife, who passed away shortly after the home was built. Julian was heartbroken and fell ill himself, eventually dying a few years later. The home sat vacant for a while and was eventually turned into a mental hospital known as Huff Sanitarium from 1944 until 1973. After the hospital closed, witnesses reported seeing patients in white gowns looking out the windows and sometimes strolling along the expansive lawn. George Julian, in life a strict Quaker, has also been spotted, staring with disdain at those who use foul language near his former home.

The Briggs family bought an Italian Renaissance-influenced home in Irvington in 1984. They didn't know the house was already occupied by the caring and kind ghost of Mrs. Johnston. The Johnston family moved into the home in the mid-fifties. Mr. Johnston died there in 1973, and Mrs. Johnston also died there a few years later. Before Don and Dawn Briggs moved in, the house had been occupied by several families. None of them ever stayed very long.

The most well-known story of the Briggs home involves one of those families. Their child suffered from an illness that required braces on each leg in order to walk. She had been put down for a nap in her upstairs bedroom, along with her younger sibling, when a scarf, left haphazardly on a lamp, caught on fire. The mother was outside hanging laundry when she saw smoke billowing out the bedroom window. She dropped the wet clothes and ran inside to rescue her children. To her utter amazement, she found the little girl sitting at the bottom of the stairs, leg braces buckled firmly on her legs, along with the toddler who was not yet walking. After extinguishing the fire, the mother returned to her little girl and asked her how they had gotten downstairs all by themselves. The child guilessly replied, "The lady brought us down."

It didn't take long for the Briggs family to realize that there was something extraordinary about their house. Footsteps heard walking up and down the wooden stairs and electrical problems were just a few of the incidents that occurred. Their young son began to talk to and play with an imaginary friend named Joe. A few years later, they learned that Mrs. Johnston had a young son named Joe who had died in the home at an early age. Dawn noticed that whenever she was in the upstairs bathtub, footsteps would steadily tread back and forth in front of the bathroom door. She would get out of the water, open the door, and the hallway would be empty. It happened so often that she eventually stopped checking the hall. She also noticed that if she loudly called, "It's O.K., Mrs. Johnston!" the noises would immediately stop.

Her husband, Don, was reluctant to believe that anything paranormal was happening. His job frequently required overnight travel, and he never witnessed any of the incidents that had plagued his wife. After a particularly exhausting day of restoration and remodeling work, the couple was leaving the house for a well-deserved dinner. As their car pulled out the driveway, Dawn thought back over the electrical problems they had experienced all afternoon. She turned to her husband and said, "Are you sure you still don't believe the stories about our house?" Don replied with a resounding, "No." At that moment, every electrical light in and on their house began to flash. They sat in the driveway, amazed, as the lights on the first floor lit up, and then the second, creating a rolling blackout effect. The pattern then went from left to right, over and over again. From that moment on, Don never again believed that his family was the only presence in his home.

Our investigation turned up several interesting items, mainly orbs. The upstairs bathroom was fairly active, and an orb was photographed hovering above the large tub. The adjacent hallway and the entrance to what used to be Mrs. Johnston's sewing room were also active. Keri and I also managed to individually photograph an orb on the outside of the house. Though faint, the orb was captured by two different makes and models of cameras and from different angles. Another picture showed a more distinct orb above the carriage lights near the front door. Perhaps Mrs. Johnston is welcoming us inside.

The Briggs family has felt the presence of ghosts in their home in Irvington. A photograph of the exterior of the house captured an orb.

CHAPTER 11

Haunted Day Trips

(Keri Young)

Indianapolis is not the only Indiana town to host ghosts. All over the state, tales of specters abound. In our years of paranormal investigating, Lorri and I have traveled to hundreds of reportedly haunted spots. Some stories have turned out to be just that, stories. While other ghostly tales paled in comparison to what we really found there. This chapter includes a few of our favorite haunted day trips. All are open to the public so take a trip if you dare.

STORY, INDIANA

The Story Inn
66 miles south of Indianapolis

Tucked into the scenic Brown County hills, the secluded town of Story is a throwback to another time. As you drive the winding desolate two-lane road through groves of thick trees and fields of soybeans and corn, you can feel yourself slipping back in time.

Dr. George Story founded the town in south-central Indiana in 1851 and built the first structure, a two-story home for himself on the highest bluff overlooking the town. One by one, others followed, creating a small building boom. Slowly the town built up as families moved to Story and more retail shops and services opened up along the main street to serve the growing community.

In the late 1800s and early 1900s, Story was the largest settlement in Brown County, and its booming population supported two general stores, a church, a one-room schoolhouse, a grain mill, a saw mill, a slaughterhouse, and a post office. For a time, life was good in Story, but then the Depression came. Little by little, Story lost its townspeople to the bigger cities as folks moved to find jobs and a better way of life.

The demise of the Story community echoed what was happening all over America during the Depression and the decade that followed. Small towns were losing their populations, and stores and businesses were forced to shutter their storefronts.

What was bad for Story then is Story's saving grace now. As people and businesses left, they closed the stores, abandoned the houses, and moved on, leaving the town exactly as it was at the time. No new construction or renovations were done, and very few structures were torn down. Story is today as it was more than one hundred years ago, stuck somewhere in the early 1900s. Story has been called the best preserved example of a nineteenth-century small town that survives in the Midwest, and for the price of an overnight stay, you can call Story home.

Today, the town of Story has been turned into a bed-and-breakfast business, the Story Inn. The remaining town buildings have all been turned into guest quarters, and the twenty-three acres of grounds offer guests plenty of room for strolling, hiking, or biking. You can spend the night over the grain mill, in Doc Story's house, above the general store, or in a number of the formerly abandoned townspeople's homes.

The former general store, with its weather-beaten trim, tin ceiling, and original gas pumps out front, is the hub of the property. It houses the check-in desk, four guest rooms, a tavern with an outdoor patio, and a gourmet restaurant where a few of the ghosts hang out.

Several ghosts are said to make Story home, but the most famous is the Blue Lady of Story. She has a room named for her above the general store at the top of the stairs, and those brave enough can test their will by turning on the blue glass lamp beside the bed. It is said this will summon the Blue Lady, and she just might pay you a visit during the night. Guest books that have been left in the room since the 1970s are filled with tales of ghostly encounters with the lady. She has been known to pinch the backside of sleeping guests, blow cold air kisses, and open and close doors. One guest awoke one early morning to find the Blue Lady staring at her from the foot of the bed. Another caught a glimpse of the lady in the large oval mirror over the bureau.

One of the owners found an old photo in the inn's attic of a woman in long, flowing white robes and an unusual blue tint to her skin. Could this be a photo of the Blue Lady? No one knows, and no one knows who the lady was. Some think she was one of Doc Story's wives; others think she might be a young wife who lived her best days here in Story with her husband before he was killed in an accident. Whoever she was, she is gentle in spirit, and her antics are always benign in nature.

The Blue Lady is not always content to stay in her room; ghostly happenings go on all over the inn and property. Diners at the gourmet restaurant on the ground floor of the inn have been known to experience the attentions of the Blue Lady. A somewhat common occurrence is the sudden breaking of glasses on the dining tables when no one is touching them. Candles have been inexplicable extinguished in front of diners' eyes, and lights have gone off and on. Employees have heard voices and movement in the deserted dining room when they are cleaning up in the kitchen.

Employees don't like to be alone in the Story Still, the cellar tavern. One employee told of cleaning up the bar area alone one night when he heard someone come down the stairs into the bar area. He thought it was another employee so he didn't even look up. He just said, "I'll be done in a minute." When he finished what he was doing, he looked up, and no one was there.

A male spirit is said to roam Doc Story's former home. Guests staying in the house have felt watched, heard phantom footsteps going up and down the stairs, and voices coming from an empty porch. Frequently, the smell of strong cherry tobacco permeates the upstairs rooms. Cleaning staff have heard their names called out and have been pinched.

I investigated the Story Inn with other paranormal investigators from the Indianapolis chapter of the Indiana Ghost Trackers. We were warmly welcomed by the inn's owner. He was quick to point out that although he doesn't fully believe in the ghost stuff, he can't discount the stories of guests and employees alike who truly believe they have encountered something. He said the inn and grounds were all ours for the night, and we eagerly broke up into groups to start trying to find evidence.

My group went down to the cellar to check out the Story Still and do some preliminary tests. While one of the investigators was alone behind the bar, he heard a distinct male voice say, "You," and then sigh. He swore no one else was around him, and he seemed quite shaken up. We took photos in the area and captured tiny orbs scattered along the ceiling. But try as we might, no one else heard any voices.

We moved from the cellar to the grounds. Behind the inn is an authentic 1901 barn now used for picturesque weddings and concerts. A sensitive investigator who was with us started to feel uneasy when we approached the barn. She said that she felt we were being watched, and it wasn't a welcoming feeling. We entered the barn on high alert for anything that might not want us there. The atmosphere felt charged. A wedding had taken place in the barn the night before, and streamers and dropped flowers littered the sawdust floor. Even those of us who were not sensitive felt uneasy. We had heard that someone in another group before us had felt that a young man had hanged himself from the biggest rafter in the barn.

We did some EVP under the rafter and upon playback heard a faint pleading, drawn-out "Nooooooooo." Nothing else was captured in the barn, so we moved on. On our way back to the inn, we passed the garden, and someone stopped the group and said that they had heard whispers as we were passing a grove of thick lilac bushes.

Our group next went to spend some time in the notorious Blue Lady Room. We turned on the blue lamp and waited in the dark. We called to the spirit to show herself and left a sheet of paper and a pencil on the bed in case she wanted to contact us. Unfortunately, nothing happened. The Blue Lady did not pay us a visit that night, but my group concluded that the inn and grounds definitely had a spirit or spirits present. And even though the Blue Lady Room is the most famous spot for ghosts at the property, we concluded that the barn area is actually the most haunted. So the next time you are in Brown County for the changing of the leaves, stop in the little town of Story for some great banana-walnut pancakes and take a walk around back. You just might have a story about Story.

BATTLE GROUND, INDIANA

Tippecanoe Battlefield Park
68 miles northwest of Indianapolis

There is a patch of land in Battle Ground, Indiana, that is saturated with blood and sorrow. The anger and fighting was so fierce, that the atmosphere is still charged with emotions and energy more than one hundred years later. Battle Ground was the site of the most important battle to take place within Indiana territory, a battle marked not only by the settlers' victory but also by the crushing of the Native American resistance. After this defeat, the Native American tribes were not able to regain the momentum for a multi-tribe fighting force.

The seeds of battle were first planted in 1808, when two Shawnee brothers would unite the Native American tribes of the area and bring them together to live in one strategic centralized settlement near Lafayette called Prophet's Town. Tecumseh and his brother Tenskwatawa, the Prophet, hoped that Prophets' Town would be a place where the tribes could come together to meet and strategize on how to push back the encroaching settlers. It would also be a place for battle training for the Native American forces who hoped to take on the settlers in an eventual battle for lands.

Settlers in the region began to feel uneasy about a large group of armed and trained Native Americans living in their midst. The governor of the Indiana Territory at the time, William Henry Harrison, was called upon by those in Washington to raise an army to drive out the ever-increasing population of Prophet's Town. On November 6, 1811, Harrison sent a representative to talk with the Prophet, and they agreed that no hostile actions would be taken by either side until a meeting could be arranged for the next day. But the Prophet did not keep his word, and shortly before dawn on November 7, the Native Americans attacked Harrison's camp.

In persuading his warriors to attack, the Prophet said he had a vision in which the Great Spirit told him if he chanted during the battle, it would make the Native American fighters impervious to the settlers' bullets. As the bloodshed began, the Prophet watched it all from a rock high above the combatants. He sang out his chant, but his vision was wrong, and the settlers' bullets cut down many Native Americans. When the two-hour battle was over, the Native Americans were defeated. It is not known how many Native Americans died during the battle, but sixty-two of Harrison's men died, and another 126 were wounded. The battlefield was littered with bodies, blood, spent arrows, and bullets.

After the defeat, the Native Americans abandoned Prophet's Town and ostracized the Prophet. Harrison's men destroyed the village, and the Native Americans gave up all hope of raising a resistance to settler occupation. There would be no united Native American force. The leaders for both sides did not go on to fulfill their dreams after this battle. The Prophet was an outcast the rest of his life and died in shame in a Shawnee village in Mississippi, and his brother Tecumseh never fulfilled his dream of uniting the Native American nations and died in battle in 1812. Harrison rose in the political ranks, ultimately becoming president in 1840. He would die of pneumonia two weeks after his inauguration, the shortest presidency in history.

The battlefield where the two sides fought so bravely is now a National Historic Landmark and commemorated by an eighty-five-foot-high marble obelisk monument. The battlefield is just a part of the ninety-six-acre Tippecanoe Battlefield Park. There are also hiking trails, a historic chapel, nature center, battle museum, gift shop, and picnic shelters.

The battle has been over for two hundred years but late at night, when the moon is full, those that live adjacent to the battlefield have been awakened by war cries and the sounds of gunfire. Teenagers walking through the grounds have sworn they heard a Native American chant coming from the hills above. People driving by the park in the early-morning hours have told of dark shapes moving through the trees. One man who lived on the perimeter of the park said one morning he was leaving for his job before dawn. It was just beginning to get light, and there was a thick fog hanging in the air. His was the only car on the road, and as he passed the battlefield, he couldn't believe his eyes. He saw shapes moving through the fog; Shapes that looked like they were engaged in battle. There were no details to the shapes; they looked like they were made of the fog itself.

Lorri and I had permission to visit the battlefield after dark on the anniversary of the battle. As we gathered our equipment in the parking lot, I looked out at the moonlit expanse of green grass and dark trees. It was eerily quiet, and the moonshine reflected brightly off the white stones that marked where each man had fallen on the battlefield. If you let your imagination run away with you, it would be easy to get caught up in the moment and spook yourself. At this point, we didn't know if the park was haunted, but it was definitely charged with some sort of energy.

We did a sweep of the park to take photos and get an idea of where we would want to set up the video camera and other equipment. As we walked along the edge of the battlefield on a ridge above the small stream, I stopped in my tracks and asked suddenly, "Lorri, do you hear that? Was that the sound of drums?" For just a few seconds I thought I might have heard the faint beat of drums. We didn't have our recorders on then so there is no evidence to verify this, but the area near the stream made the hairs on the back of my neck stand at attention.

We did EVP in the middle of the battleground, calling out to specific soldiers who had lost their lives that day in 1811. We took digital pictures, video, and temperature readings but could find nothing unusual. We had great hopes for getting clear EVP on the anniversary of the battle using specific names, but upon playback, we didn't get anything.

We moved our equipment down the road a little bit to Prophet's Rock, the spot high up on the ridge where the Prophet was supposed to have watched the battle and sang out his chant of protection. We climbed up the well-worn rocks to the top where there is a big flat rock that looked like it could be the one he sat upon. We had brought limited equipment up there since we had to climb up a steep incline, but we did have our recorders and digital cameras. We got some faint inaudible sounds and some large orbs in a few photos, but nothing conclusive.

While not much evidence was collected on our trip to the battlefield, it's definitely a unique place with its own energy. And because there are so many eyewitness accounts of activity in and around the battlefield, this area warrants further investigation.

CHESTERFIELD, INDIANA

Camp Chesterfield
50 miles north of Indianapolis

The religion of Spiritualism began with two sisters in 1848. The Fox sisters of upstate New York said they could communicate with the dead, and during their séances, the dead would knock in response to questions. Their séances became so popular that they took their show on the road, giving psychic readings and producing talking spirits in wealthy homes all over the Northeast. As newspapers started featuring the sisters on their front pages, their popularity grew, and soon they were conducting séances for larger and larger audiences all over the country. Other mediums noted their success and copied the Foxes, giving their own public séances and readings all over the world.

The Spiritualist movement evolved from these early séances. Spiritualism is the science, philosophy, and religion of continuous life based upon communication by means of mediumship with those of the spirit world. During the late 1800s, spiritualism became so popular that mediums set up spiritualist camps all over the U. S. and Europe where the audiences would come to them. The faithful could camp or stay in hotels built on the grounds to attend lectures, séances, classes, and worship services.

Camp Chesterfield in Chesterfield, Indiana, was one of the largest and most popular of these camps. Founded in 1886 on land donated by the Bronnenbergs, a German immigrant family, Camp Chesterfield became a popular summer destination for folks hoping to rest, relax, and communicate with the dead.

As the popularity of the camp increased, temporary tents that had been housing the guests, mediums, and places of worship were replaced with permanent buildings. The grounds would soon include a cathedral, museum, administration building, cafeteria, three hotels, a chapel, homes, and gardens and trails.

In the camp's heyday, thousands of customers were coming to talk to their departed loved ones. The camp mediums offered all the popular services of the day—trumpeting, flame throwing, trance, psychic artistry, and materializations, among others. The cathedral housed lively and packed services, and the camp showcased readings by

Spiritualist celebrities. The grounds were always bustling with one event or another.

The camp and mediums prospered until the Spiritualist movement lost momentum in the early twentieth century. Many of the camps around the world were forced to close when the faithful stopped coming. Believers are still out there, but in smaller numbers. Camp Chesterfield has felt the decline in attendance and now needs only one hotel. It is one of only a handful of the Spiritualist camps that have been able to survive.

Today the camp's busiest events are psychic readings on the first Saturday of each month. People start lining up two hours before opening for the chance to sit with one of the camp's best mediums. On any given first Saturday you might get a reading from a palmist, trance medium, aura reader, tarot-card reader, or trumpeter.

If you can't wait for the first Saturday, you can visit Medium's Row, which is the street of historic cottages built for the resident mediums. Each tiny house has a plaque outside stating the mediums' specialty and hours they are available. Don't miss the interesting art gallery, museum, and bookstore for an in-depth look at Spiritualism, or take a scenic walk on either the Trail of Religions or the Serenity Walk.

The mediums are a very closed society, and it was hard to find specific ghost stories about the property. We had heard over and over, "Camp Chesterfield is creepy," "There is something haunting the camp," and "That place gives me the creeps." But no one could tell us what specifically was haunting the camp. We did hear a story about the back of the property, near the Totem Garden. A little boy's spirit plays tricks on passersby. He moves things that are set down, laughs, and throws small pebbles—nothing harmful, just mischievous. The hotel is also supposed to be haunted by a spirit who opens and shuts doors, turns out the lights, and leaves the water running.

Lorri and I visited the grounds on several occasions, the first while attending Spirit Fest, a fall festival featuring mediums, retailers, classes, and lectures, and then on several other investigations. At Spirit Fest, we walked around the grounds with a sketch pad and drew a rough map of the grounds, marking an X on areas we wanted to investigate further on a less crowded day. We tried interviewing the resident mediums but were not very successful in getting them to open up about the hauntings at the camp. They were all very nice, but seemed very reluctant to talk about ghosts with outsiders. Just when we thought our day was a bust, a man cautiously approached us and said if we wanted to know about ghosts to meet him in the museum in fifteen minutes. We were intrigued. We wrapped up our walk through the grounds, took some photos, visited the festival booths, and kept our mysterious appointment.

When we met George in the museum, he told us he had been a former medium at the camp and had fallen out of favor with the administration. He told us that we would never get anyone to tell us about the ghosts because the mediums don't trust outsiders; they had been burned one too many times. But he said the camp was full of spirits. "By the nature of what we do, communicating with the dead, it stands to reason that some would want to hang around in a place where they can be heard. We attract spirits here," He explained.

Lorri asked if there were particular places on which we should concentrate when we investigate. "Try the hotel. There are supposed to be several [spirits] there. They turn on the faucets, move things about, walk up and down the stairs loudly, and tug on the blankets," he said. "There is also a part of the grounds near the totem pole that gives off radiant energy. The ghost of a little boy is supposed to have been seen there, but I haven't seen him myself." George talked more about the camp and started heating up about the politics of the camp, skeptics, and other issues. We were only interested in the ghosts, so we thanked him and left for the day.

During subsequent investigative visits, we used dowsing rods around the property, and they reacted strongly in the area around the totem pole, near the back of the cathedral, and near the river. When we got a strong dowsing rod signal, we took pictures in rapid succession. The totem pole area was very active with orbs of varying size. One of the largest orbs was red, which some paranormal experts think is a sign of negative energy. We couldn't get in the hotel without renting a room. Lorri and I plan to do just that on our next trip to see what kind of evidence we could gather there.

Camp Chesterfield is an interesting place, one of the few like it left in the U. S. If you get a chance to visit, the museum alone is worth the drive.

FRENCH LICK, INDIANA

French Lick Springs Resort and Casino
105 miles south of Indianapolis

In the mid 1800s, mineral-springs resorts were all the rage throughout the U. S. and Europe. Drinking and bathing in the warm mineral-infused waters from natural springs was a popular cure all for all that ailed you. Mineral-springs purveyors exalted the curing properties of the water to remedy everything from gout to wrinkles. Capitalizing on this fad, Dr. William Bowles bought 1,500 acres that included several large mineral springs in French Lick, Indiana, and opened the French Lick Springs Hotel in 1845. People came from all over the country to sample the waters, and the hotel prospered. Dr. Bowles ran the hotel until his death in 1873. The hotel continued to be managed by a series of owners until 1897, when it nearly burned to the ground.

The French Lick Hotel Co., headed by then Indianapolis Mayor Thomas Taggart, bought the hotel ruins and rebuilt the hotel bigger and better than before. His political clout enabled him to persuade the railroad to lay tracks practically to the hotel's front door, allowing quick and easy access from Chicago, Indianapolis, and every other major city around the country. The public ate it up. The two trains a day that came into French Lick were filled to capacity with well-heeled guests just salivating to "take some of the waters."

The French Lick Springs Hotel had it all—natural mineral springs, championship golf, baseball, pools, a spa, dancing, gambling, drinking, and fine dining. In 1914, the world-famous chef Louis Perrin first served tomato juice as a beverage there. Life was good at the French Lick Springs Hotel.

Taggart's position as Democratic national chairman brought movie stars and important political figures to the tiny town of French Lick. With all the noted Democratic big wigs floating around it, the hotel gained a reputation as the unofficial Democratic national headquarters. So much so, that Franklin Roosevelt held a large fund-raiser at the hotel to raise money for his 1931 presidential bid.

Thomas Taggart died in 1929, and his son Tom took over hotel leadership. The hotel weathered tough times during the Depression years, but eked by with conventions and golf getaways. The year 1949 would mark an end to Taggart ownership of the hotel. Since then, the hotel has been run by various corporations with varying degrees of success. In 2006, the hotel underwent a $382 million restoration, bringing it back to its glory days.

Just as in Taggart's days, the resort has fine dining, a world-class spa, two pools, bowling, and two championship golf courses. The addition of a casino between the French Lick Springs Hotel and the West Baden Springs Hotel has brought excitement back to the valley.

A hotel that has been around for more than 150 years is bound to have some ghosts, right? The French Lick Springs Hotel has had documented paranormal happenings since the Taggart era, and some even involve Taggart himself.

Back in his day, Taggart would ride his horse down the long hallway between the lobby and the ballroom in the slow winter months. Today, guests are sometimes flabbergasted to hear the sounds of an invisible horse trotting down the hallways late at night. A few have run to the front desk saying they saw the misty outline of a horse and rider. The staff, many of whom have had the same experiences, always reassure them that it's just the hotel's beloved patriarch.

Taggart was a hands-on owner of the hotel and would often hold the elevators for guests, all the while smoking his trademark cigars. There is an elevator at the hotel that opens for guests before they call it, and sometimes mysteriously the elevator goes to the guests' floor before they push the button. The smell of pipe tobacco still lingers in the elevator when no one is there. The staff believes this is Taggart still being helpful. This same elevator is known to go up and down the floors in the middle of the night when no one has pushed the call buttons.

The sixth floor is known for cold drafts, odd noises, the tinkling of glass, misty amorphous shapes, shadows along the hallway, and the sounds of footsteps when the hallway is empty. The cleaning crew is reluctant to go to that floor at night because of an unseen presence that watches them while they work.

There is something or someone in a room on the sixth floor that likes to call the front desk, even when no one is registered to that room. For many years, especially in the dead of winter, the front desk will see a call coming in from that room. When the call is picked up, there is nothing on the line but static. After the employee hangs up, the room sometimes calls back with the same static response. One employee said, "I was standing near the operator late one night when a call came in from that room. I had never answered the phone for that room so she handed me the phone. There was just silence and then static. No sound, just crackling. I kept saying, "Hello," but there was no answer. I hung up the phone and felt really creepy. Then the room called back. I never answered if that room called again."

At the end of the hallway on the sixth floor is the bloody honeymoon suite, a room so haunted that several guests staying in that room have fled in the middle of the night. In the 1940s, a couple checked into the room on their honeymoon. Late that night, something went horribly wrong. The man hanged himself with bed covers from his window. When security kicked in the door to get to him, he was already dead. They found his wife also dead in the bathtub. She had been stabbed hundreds of times, and the water ran red with her blood. It was concluded to be a murder-suicide.

Staff said that the bathtub in the room had a rust-colored stain that could never be cleansed away. They tried bleach and scouring, and it would disappear for a while but return days later. During the renovation the bathtub was replaced. Time will tell if the stain returns.

On the first floor, in between an area that used to be called the Governor's Suite and the President's Suite, Taggart's daughter killed herself at the bottom of a spiral stairway. The stairway is no longer there but the dark red stain remains. A maintenance worker told us, "The stain is still there. We just replaced the carpet in that area about six months ago. We have scrubbed that stain away countless times. It keeps returning. Now we don't even try." There are hundreds of other ghost sightings and odd occurrences at the hotel, but they are all benign. The atmosphere is one of happiness and excitement.

Lorri and I have investigated the hotel on numerous occasions. In our opinion, it's one of the most haunted properties we have ever stepped foot in. The staff at the hotel is exceptionally great. They went out of their way to get us all the ghostly tales and hooked us up with eye witnesses in some cases. Here are a few of the paranormal anomalies that have occurred to both Lorri and I during our many stays at the hotel:

Photographs of the garden at the French Lick Springs Resort and Casino reveal a number of orbs.

The witching hour is said to be 1:00 A.M., and it is the time when supernatural creatures such as ghosts are thought to be at their most powerful. Coincidentally, or not, that happened to be when Lorri and I got some of our best results. So, with backpacks filled with equipment, we set forth to cover all areas of the hotel. We had the hotel to ourselves, and management had given us unprecedented access from the very top to the basement and grounds.

We wanted to cover the known hot spots first, so we proceeded to the infamous sixth floor. As we crossed the lobby toward the elevator, its doors opened before we had a chance to push a button. We got in, not knowing what to expect. We waited for the button for our floor to be mysteriously pushed, but it wasn't.

Before the renovation in 2006, the hallways of the French Lick Springs Hotel were almost exactly like the hallways in the hotel from *The Shining*—twenty-four-foot-tall ceilings and long, dark, deserted hallways—a ghost hunters dream. Now, the hallways are brightly lit and there are more guests, making it hard to capture orb images or EVP, but there are still ghostly happenings going on masked by the brightness.

Our first investigation point was the bloody honeymoon suite. We took photos down the hallway towards the room. The photo showed a web of orbs blocking our path and covering the hallway from floor to ceiling. It was amazing. We had to walk through the orbs, but didn't feel anything as we headed toward our destination. Unfortunately the rooms were reserved, but we stood outside and did EVP recordings and took EMF meter readings. The meter spiked every few minutes and then fell silent. At one point Lorri noticed a cold draft coming from somewhere. The hotel's constant temperature was on the warm side so this sudden coldness was interesting. We tried to find a source for the air, but could find none that we had access to. When we played the EVP recordings back, there was a man's laughter on the tape— laughter that we had not heard while we were standing there.

We got a tip from hotel security that said we should also check out the seventh floor. They said that recently they were called up to the seventh floor because a guest had complained about a room-service cart loudly going up and down the hallway while the guest was try- ing to sleep. Security talked to the kitchen; no cart had been sent.

On the seventh floor, we set out meters and cameras and were concentrating on one end of the hallway when suddenly the small door on the other end, which led to the roof, opened slowly. I wanted to make sure no one was playing a trick on us. Lorri investigated the area and said, "No one is on the roof, and there is not any air to blow the door open." We could not provide an answer as to how the door swung open. On another trip to the seventh floor, both Lorri and I smelled cigar smoke. We can't be certain someone in their room wasn't smoking, but it seemed more likely that Thomas Taggart was paying us a visit.

At 3:00 A.M., most of the hotel was asleep. We sat with the few remaining front-desk staff and asked to hear more haunted stories about the hotel. One longtime front-desk associate said that Taggart had built his son a mini mansion on Mount Aire, the highest point in French Lick and on the farthest end of the hotel's property. She said, "That house has been used for years as the residence of the hotel's manager, and it's supposed to be more haunted than the hotel itself. My aunt was a seamstress for the hotel and in the 1970s was called out to the mansion to repair the drapes. She was left alone in the house and was upstairs hemming the drapes when she heard the front door open and close [and] footsteps that walked up the stairs and down the hall toward her. Then the steps just stopped. She turned around expecting to see the owner or some other staff member. There was no one there. She fled the house, leaving the pins in the drapes."

Just then the bell on the other end of the check-in counter dinged all by itself. We took that as a good sign. Ghosts check in, but they don't check out.

LEAVENWORTH, INDIANA

Wyandotte Caves
147 miles south of Indianapolis

In the mid and late 1800s, caves were a fascinating and popular destination for tourists in the U. S. Wyandotte Caves in southern Indiana opened to the public in 1851 and became an instant success. The caves became so popular that the owner, Henry Rothrock, opened a hotel on the property and added more tour guides. As the dollars came in, more and more of the cave was explored, and new areas opened up for additional tours. The Rothrock family continued to own and operate the property until 1966, when it was sold to the state of Indiana, which then made improvements, added lights, and kept the tours going. Today, the caves are located in the more than twenty-four-thousand-acre Harrison Crawford/Wyandotte Woods State Forest with more than nine miles of explored caves to see. There are two tours offered—the Flowstone Falls and Monument Mountain tours—and a small interpretive museum is also on site.

During the winter months, the caves are closed due to the more than three hundred thousand bats that hibernate inside. The Indiana bat and six other endangered species of bats spend the winter months hanging upside down in the solitude and darkness of the cave.

According to legend, it's not only the bats that lurk in the dark. There are two ghost stories connected with the cave. It is said that Henry Rothrock needed to hire some temporary help to work in the cave to widen the tunnels for the public walkways. He hired three odd fellows who said they could only work at night. Finding it strange but needing the work done in a hurry, Rothrock hired the men, and for several weeks they worked every night in the cave, only seeing Rothrock to get their paychecks. All went well until a tour guide exploring on his own found a large crate in a passageway not open to the public. He told his boss, and Rothrock went down to the passageway and broke open the crate. It held a printing press to make U.S. currency. The workers had been down in the cave printing money. Rothrock immediately alerted the police who waited for them above ground on the next payday. When the trio came out of the cave and saw the police, they started running. Two were immediately captured, but one ran back down into the cave. The police went in after him, but he was never found. They posted guards at the entranceway but the counterfeiter never came out. It is thought he must have died somewhere in the cave. Since then, many a tourist has thought he saw the shadow of a man down in the caves. Sometimes they alert guards that someone has broken away from the group and is wandering alone. When the guides go to look, no one is found. Calls for help have also echoed the vast passages where no earthly person has been.

Rothrock had a young son named Andrew whose favorite thing in the world was exploring and playing in the caves with his father. He came home from school every day and immediately went down into the caves until it was time for supper. He did this for years until one summer he started feeling ill. His family took him to doctor after doctor, but no one could find out exactly what was wrong with young Andrew. When he was at his weakest and there looked like no hope for a recovery, his family took him down to the cave for one last visit. Not long after that he succumbed to his illness.

When the tour guides turn out the lights in the mountain room to demonstrate how dark a cave can be and then light their lanterns again, there is often a gasp as someone in the crowd sees the shape of a boy reflected on the other side of the mountain of rock, a side that cannot be reached anymore due to collapsing sheets of rock. Many think this is Andrew playing with the crowd.

I took a trip to Wyandotte Caves in the summer but had no special permission to hunt in the cave. The government almost never grants permission to any of its properties, so I took the Monument Mountain

Hundreds of orbs are visible in photographs of the mountain room in Wyandotte Caves in Leavenworth, Indiana.

tour with the rest of the crowds. It was an interesting tour, and I loved that there were still a few furry little bats hanging just inches over our heads. "Don't make any sudden movements," the tour guide said, "or you will panic them all and they will come flying out in one big group." I did not have a chance to use meters or try to get EVP. I did photograph hundreds of orbs of varying density in the mountain room, but I cannot be certain if they were the ghosts of Andrew or the counterfeiter or perhaps just dust kicked up from all the tourists.

MITCHELL, INDIANA

Whispers Estate Bed and Breakfast
85 miles south of Indianapolis

On a main street in the southern Indiana town of Mitchell, there is a big white mansion that no one will speak about. Built in 1899 by Dr. John Gibbons, the large Victorian was both a home for his family and the site of his office and operating room. Today, the 3,200-square-foot home has been turned into the Whispers Estate Bed and Breakfast by proprietor Jarret Marshall. Some say the Gibbons family never left.

Marshall bought the long-neglected Gibbons home in 2004 and immediately began renovating and restoring it with assistance from family members. When he bought the house he never intended to open a bed-and-breakfast. It was only after the whispers and other strange things started happening that Marshall thought there might be a market for a bed-and-breakfast-and-ghost establishment.

Marshall's first task for the renovation was to tear down a partition wall that had been put up between the parlor and the entry hall. In the basement, he found two large square pillars that fit perfectly into the newly created space. After he installed the first pillar, there was a pounding on the front door. Marshall could see the door shaking with violent knocking but when he went to open it, there was no one there. This was a sign of things to come.

After the pillars were reinstalled in their original spot, the whispers, footsteps, and other events started. Any time of day, whispering could be heard, and after all were in bed and the house was quiet, tiny feet were heard running up and down the wooden floors. Marshall knew that Dr. Gibbons built the home for his wife, Jessie, daughter, Rachel, and son, Ennis, in 1899 and that the family had lived in the home until the doctor's death in 1934, but the curious events made Marshall want to know more.

In researching the history of the old home, Marshall found resistance from neighbors and town residents. No one wanted to talk about the Gibbons family, and some even said the past was best left in the past. But Marshall persisted and found an old newspaper article that shed light on the paranormal events going on at his house. "Mitchell Girl Dies in Christmas Day Fire" read the headline of a small article. It went on to say that Dr. John Gibbon's twelve-year-old daughter, Rachel, was killed in a tragic fire on Christmas Day 1912. She had been alone in the parlor of her home and backed into the Christmas tree, which had been festooned with lit candles. Her dress caught fire, and in her panic she could not open the pocket doors to get help and was consumed by the fire.

Additional research yielded that the girl's mother was inconsolable after Rachel's death, and she rarely left her room on the top floor. Tragedy struck again two years later when the couple's only son, Ennis, died. Jessie spiraled into a deep depression and a series of ailments. She contracted pneumonia when she was thirty-six years old and never recovered. Her official cause of death was pneumonia but everyone knew it was from a broken heart.

After the doctor's death, the house passed to relatives and eventually became a rooming house for decades before it was converted back to a single-family home. Now knowing the history, Marshall believes his house is still a home for the Gibbons family, and he wants to share this otherworldly experience with others.

The bed-and-breakfast features five bedrooms, all elegantly appointed and one with a private bath. There is Rachel's room, the servants' quarters, the master bedroom, and what was formerly the doctor's office and surgery room. Paranormal activity has been experienced in every room of the house, but each spirit seems to have his or her favorite.

Marshall says Rachel's is the strongest presence. "She runs around the hallways and upstairs rooms at night with bare feet. I would say that is the one thing most people experience." She also likes to play and move objects around. She is the most audible and has been heard singing on several occasions.

The mother, Jessie, is also present and is often heard shushing her exuberant daughter or seen walking about. The doctor is in residence, but his presence is smelled more often than seen. When the doctor is around, there is a strong smell of aftershave. The scent will come and go and sometimes follow you from room to room, growing stronger until it almost chokes you, but his is not as prevalent as the female spirits. The little boy is very rarely seen or felt, and only sensitives or true psychics have been able to sense his presence.

Lorri and I stumbled on to the information about Whispers Estates as we were researching for another chapter. But after a quick phone call, we were invited down to the estate by Marshall, who turned out to be an excellent host, cook, and historian. When we arrived we got acquainted in the parlor that had been the scene of poor Rachel's demise. Marshall showed us the original pocket door that still had extensive scorching and black burn marks.

As we sat in the dimmed parlor, Marshall told us the history of the Gibbons family, the tragedies, and what paranormal events have been experienced there. While he was talking, I suddenly became aware that it was becoming harder and harder for me to breathe. There was a slight pressure on my chest, and at the same time my eyes filled with tears. I was taken aback by this unexpected emotional reaction. I stopped Marshall in midsentence and said, "Hey, guys, don't think I'm crazy, but I am finding it hard to breathe, and my eyes are tearing up." Marshall said, "You're not crazy. Several people have had that same reaction in this room. You may be tapping into the feelings Rachel had that day." I have never had such an uncontrolled emotional reaction in any haunted location. This was going to be an interesting night.

Marshall said, "There has been activity in every room of this house. In the parlor, faces have been seen staring in at us, cold hands have touched people's ankles, and there's the smell of smoke and burning wood. In the doctor's former surgery room, which is now a bedroom, I was sleeping one night when I awoke at 10:30 and a dark figure came out of the bathroom and leaned over me. That happened several nights in a row, always at the same time. I warn folks who stay in that room to be prepared at 10:30 P.M."

Rachel's room has the most activity. Guests sleeping in that room have felt a small child get in bed with them, and when the lights are turned on, no one is there. They have also had dolls and other toys tucked in with them while they slept. A lot of people bring toys to leave for Rachel, and sometimes they are scattered around the room in the morning as if Rachel had played with them in the night.

The upstairs bathroom has had occurrences, too. There is a large claw-foot iron tub left over from when the house was a rooming house. "One night I came home from work, and there was a leak in the downstairs ceiling. When I traced where it was coming from, the large heavy bathtub upstairs had been turned on its side and the pipe had burst. Someone who had lived in the house when it was a rooming house said that one of the renters died in that tub. In the servants' quarters in the back of the house, people have heard whispers, the windows are taped, and someone captured an EVP of a little boy saying, "Close the door."

Marshall said he could tell us a lot more, but suggested we take a tour of the house and grounds first. We went to the backyard where he said an Indiana ghost group had discovered a remarkable find the weekend before. "They were using dowsing rods in the backyard when they started indicating that there were graves right next to the house. After they staked the area, they brought in a type of sonar equipment that confirmed that there are most probably five unmarked graves in the backyard. Two of those are of children." No one knows who is buried there, and no records can confirm burial sites. Our equipment detected a disturbance in the EMF field in the backyard as well. Marshall said the yard is something he will look into after he finishes renovating the entire house.

We went inside. It was nearly midnight, and we decided to set up our base for the investigation in the parlor. We sat quietly with the chandelier turned down low and asked Rachel to show herself. We had placed trigger objects, in this case toys, at strategic spots around the house. After we had started our EVP recording session, when Marshall asked questions to Rachel, the chandelier above us began to dim and then brighten. It did this over and over when the question was about or to Rachel. We asked directly, "Is this Rachel?" and the chandelier dimmed.

I stopped recording and asked, "Do you smell that? It smells medicinal or like minty aftershave." Lorri smelled something as she walked around the room, the scent getting stronger in some areas. We tried to find the source of the smell but couldn't. It became stronger and stronger, until the air was thick with it. Marshall said, "That's the doctor." I don't know why but those words coupled with the distinct smell sent a chill down my back. I knew there was someone unseen in the room with us.

Throughout the rest of the investigation, the cologne smell would come and go. It followed us from the parlor to the dining room and then faded away. In Rachel's room, we took careful note of the place-ment of trigger items and toys. As we left Rachel's room, Lorri's shirt was tugged by an unseen hand. When we had explored the entire house and had conducted EVP recordings in every room, we returned to the parlor to see what other events would occur.

Again in the parlor we dimmed the lights and listened. There was movement upstairs. It sounded like a trunk was being dragged across the back servants' quarters. Marshall went up to investigate but found nothing amiss. We all heard a "Shhhhhh" come from the stairs. The medicinal smell returned for a few minutes then dissipated, and the chandelier continued to grow dim and then brighten as we were talking.

One of the most interesting stories that Marshall told us was of a ghostly call to 911. At one point, he was thinking of selling the old home and had made several phone calls to realtors. Marshall said, "About thirty minutes after I had signed up with a realtor, police cars pulled up outside of the house and knocked on the door. They said they had received a 911 call from this house. But I hadn't called anyone. They wouldn't take my word for it and searched the house. They said there was a little girl screaming on the 911 call. They searched the entire house but couldn't find anything. They concluded there was something wrong with the phone lines, but I know it was Rachel saying she did not want me to sell the house."

Marshall didn't let the 911 call dissuade him, and he listed the house anyway. When a realtor brought a couple over to view the house, they asked to tour it by themselves. When they came back

A photograph captured a moving orb in the parlor of the Whispers Estate Bed and Breakfast in Mitchell, Indiana.

downstairs from taking a tour, they said, "Your daughter is really mad. She was in her room with her arms crossed and would not answer us when we said hello." Marshall had to tell them he didn't have a daughter. They went right out the front door and didn't return calls.

After we finished our investigation in the main area of the house, Lorri and I retired to our respective rooms to see what the rest of the evening had in store for us. I was staying in the doctor's office on the first floor of the house. I can say that after all the activity of the night I had a hard time falling asleep and staying asleep. Around 3:00 A.M., I heard little bare feet running outside of my door. The house was silent except for a grandfather clock, and the footsteps were distinctive. Sometime later I heard the plastic ball we had placed on the lower stair landing go rolling past my door into what I presumed was the dining room. I got up and switched on my recorder. I couldn't get up the courage to open my door and look out at what might be there. I got back into bed and tried to go back to sleep. That's when the cologne smell started again. It began slowly but really got thick and overpowering. I jumped out of bed and turned on the light; nothing was there. It was almost morning then, and I thought it wise to keep the light on until dawn. I can say this for certain: I have never had my heart race so fast on an investigation. Usually I am not sleeping in the middle of the investigation site, but never the less, this place was creepy.

The next morning over a terrific breakfast spread of fresh baked muffins and bagels, I asked Lorri if she had experienced anything during the night. She said she had not heard anything. Just then, we heard a faint moan or cry from above us. It sounded farther away than the second story; it might have come from the attic. That was a good enough sign for us that our investigation at the Whisper Estates Bed and Breakfast had come to an end. I, for one, can recommend this B&B for anyone wanting a weekend getaway filled with ghostly tales, abundant activity, and great company. Just don't go for the rest; you might not be doing much sleeping.

APPENDIX A

Sighting Report Form

Photocopy and enlarge the form on the next page to a standard 8.5 x 11 inch format. This form should be completed right after a sighting. If the ghost hunt is performed by a group, a designated leader should assume the role of reporter. The reporter is responsible for completing this form.

The reporter and each witness should make a statement, either audio or written, describing in full their experiences at the site. Date, sign, and label these statements with a reference number identical to the report number on the sighting report form. Attach the statements to the report form.

SIGHTING REPORT

SITE NAME _____ REPORT # _____
LOCATION_____ DATE: _____
_____ TIME: _____
REPORTER_____ SITE # _____
WITNESSES _____

DESCRIPTION OF APPARITION: _____

temperature change   [ ] YES   [ ] NO
auditory phenomena   [ ] YES   [ ] NO
telekinesis   [ ] YES   [ ] NO
visual phenomena   [ ] YES   [ ] NO
other phenomena   [ ] YES   [ ] NO
Description: _____

Use the reverse side for diagrams, maps, and drawings.

SPECIFIC LOCATION WITHIN SITE: _____

PREVIOUS SIGHTINGS AT THIS SITE?
                [ ] YES   [ ] NO
Reference: _____
Summary: _____

RECORDS:
audio   [ ] YES   [ ] NO   Ref. No. _____
video   [ ] YES   [ ] NO   Ref. No. _____
photo   [ ] YES   [ ] NO   Ref. No. _____
Summary of Records _____

Disposition of records: _____

WITNESS STATEMENTS (Summary): _____

audio   [ ] YES   [ ] NO
written   [ ] YES   [ ] NO
Disposition of statements: _____

Suggested Reading

BOOKS

Auerbach, Loyd. *Ghost Hunting: How to Investigate the Paranormal.* Berkeley: Ronin Publishing, 2003.

———. *Hauntings and Poltergeists.* Berkeley: Ronin Publishing, 2004.

Brandon, Trent. *The Ghost Hunter's Bible.* Galloway: Zerotime Paranormal and Supernatural Research, 2002.

Browne, Sylvia. *Visits from the Afterlife.* New York: New American Library, 2004.

Holzer, Hans. *Ghosts: True Encounters with the World Beyond.* New York: Black Dog & Leventhal, 2004.

Kaczmarek, Dale. *Field Guide to Spirit Photography.* Alton: Whitechapel Productions Press, 2002.

Konstantinos. *Contact the Other Side: Seven Methods for Afterlife Communication.* St. Paul: Llewellyn Publications, 2001.

Marimen, Mark. *Haunted Indiana.* Holt: Thunder Bay Press, 1997.

———. *Haunted Indiana 2.* Holt: Thunder Bay Press, 1999.

———. *Haunted Indiana 3.* Holt: Thunder Bay Press, 2001.

———. *Haunted Indiana 4.* Holt: Thunder Bay Press, 2005.

Mead, Robin. *Haunted Hotels: A Guide to American and Canadian Inns and Their Ghosts.* Nashville: Thomas Nelson, Inc. 1995.

Mercado, Elaine. *Grave's End: A True Ghost Story.* St. Paul: Llewellyn Publications, 2001.

Myers, Arthur. *A Ghosthunter's Guide: To Haunted Landmarks, Parks, Churches, and Other Public Places.* Chicago: Contemporary Books, 1993.

Norman, Michael, and Beth Scott. *Historic Haunted America*. New York: Tom Doherty Associates, 1995.

Ogdon, Tom. *The Complete Idiot's Guide to Ghosts and Hauntings*. New York: Alpha Books, 1999.

Ramsland, Katherine. *Ghost: Investigating the Other Side*. New York: Thomas Dunne Books, 2001.

Scott, Beth, and Michael Norman. *Haunted Heartland*. New York: Warner Books, 1987.

Taylor, Troy. *The Ghost Hunter's Guidebook*. Alton: Whitechapel Productions Press, 1999.

Thay, Edrick. *Ghost Stories of Indiana*. Edmonton: Lone Pine Publishing, 2002.

Warren, Joshua P. *How to Hunt Ghosts: A Practical Guide*. New York: Simon & Schuster, 2003.

Warren, Ed, and Lorraine Warren. *Graveyard: More Terrifying Than Stephen King - Because It's True*. New York: St. Martin's Press, 1993.

Westbie, Constance, and Harold Cameron. *Night Stalks the Mansion: A True Story of One Family's Ghostly Adventure*. Mechanicsburg: Stackpole Books, 2005.

Willis, Wanda Lou. *Haunted Hoosier Trails: A Guide to Indiana's Famous Folklore Spooky Sites*. Zionsville: Guild Press, 2002.

————. *More Haunted Hoosier Trails*. Cincinnati: Emmis Books, 2004.

ARTICLES

Cumings, Ingrid. "On the fright track." *Indianapolis Monthly*, October 2006.

Edwards, Nicole. "Haunted weekend." *Intake Weekly*, October 27, 2005.

Martinez, Kimiko L. "Circle City spooks: We shed light on Indy's darkest local lore, tall tales and frightening sightings." *Intake Weekly*, October 21, 2004.

McPhee, Laura. "Grave mistakes." *Nuvo Newsweekly*, June 28, 2006.

Quigley, Fran. "Who you gonna call?" *Nuvo Newsweekly*, October 30, 2002.

Walker, Jim. "Beyond the graveyard: Death becomes Jim during his tour at Crown Hill Cemetery." *Intake Weekly*, November 9, 2006.

APPENDIX C

Films, DVDs, and Videos

Documentaries on ghost hunting are fascinating, but because of the elusive nature of ghosts, there just aren't very many of them. Most documentaries are re-creations of past events. However, a handful do provide compelling and unexplainable recorded evidence of paranormal occurrences. Fictional movies about ghosts and haunted houses are entertaining and can also provide a glimpse, albeit a glamorized one, of more dramatic hauntings. The movie *White Noise* with Michael Keaton introduced many people to the relatively unexplored idea of electronic voice phenomenon. *The Shining* was a blockbuster horror film about a haunted hotel that scared even nonbelievers. Below is our recommended viewing list.

A Haunting in Georgia (2002). A made-for-TV movie directed by Jeffrey Fine and starring Michael Larson and Mary Barclay.
A Haunting: The Haunting of Summerwind (2006). A docudrama by the Discovery Channel. Real-life survivors describe their dramatic encounters at Summerwind, an old mansion on the shore of West Bay Lake, Wisconsin.
The Amityville Horror (1979). Directed by Stuart Rosenberg. Starring James Brolin and Margot Kidder. Based upon the book written by Jay Anson, newlyweds become affected by the legacy of brutal murders committed in their new home.
Below (2002). Directed by David Twohy. Starring Matthew Davis and Bruce Greenwood. Ghosts are everywhere, even in a World War II submarine.
Central State: Asylum for the Insane (2006). A documentary directed by

Dan T. Hall and filmed on location at Central State Mental Hospital.
The Changeling (1980). Directed by Peter Medak. Starring George C.
Scott and Trish Van Devere. A classy combination of horror and
mystery with subtle creepiness.
Children of the Grave (2007). Directed by the Booth brothers. Cast
includes Keith Age, Troy Taylor, John Zaffis, and Mary Ellen
Hammack. A documentary featuring the ghosts of children.
The Entity (1981). Directed by Sidney J. Furie. Starring Barbara
Hershey and Ron Silver. Physical assault by an unseen presence
drives a woman to seek help from parapsychologists.
Ghost Hunters: The Complete First Season (2004). Starring Jason
Hawes, Grant Wilson, Brian Harnois, Keith Johnson, and Carl
Johnson. A Sci Fi channel reality series depicting the lives of real
ghost hunters.
Ghost Story (1981). Directed by John Irving. Starring Fred Astaire
and Douglas Fairbanks Jr. Based upon Peter Straub's bestselling
horror novel, a ghost seeks revenge on four old friends who mur-
dered her many years ago.
Ghost Whisperer (2005). Network television series starring Jennifer
Love Hewitt as a young woman who sees and communicates with
earth-bound spirits.
Grave Secrets: The Legacy of Hilltop Drive (1992). Directed by John
Patterson. Starring Patty Duke. Based upon the true story of a cou-
ple who spent their life savings on a new home and discovered the
development was built upon an old graveyard.
The Grudge (2004). Directed by Takashi Shimizu. Starring Sarah
Michelle Gellar. Ghosts, Japanese style.
Haunted (1996). Directed by Lewis Gilbert. Starring Aidan Quinn
and Kate Beckinsale. Based upon the chilling novel by James
Herbert, a skeptical ghost hunter experiences unspeakable terror in
this gothic ghost story.
Haunted History: Haunted Hollywood (2007). As seen on the History
Channel. Historians and eyewitnesses recount harrowing ghost sto-
ries about some of Hollywood's most beloved actors and actresses.
The Haunting (1963). Directed by Robert Wise. Starring Julie Harris
and Claire Bloom. Based upon Shirley Jackson's novel *The
Haunting of Hill House*. A classic horror film.
Most Haunted: The Collection (2007). A Travel Channel reality series.

Ghost hunters and psychics investigate some of the scariest locations in Britain. Includes all twenty episodes from seasons one and two.

Mystic Indiana (2003). Produced by Paz Productions, narrated by Mark Marimen, and featuring members of the Indiana Ghost Trackers. Re-creations and actual footage of haunted areas in Indiana.

The Others (2002). Directed by Alejandro Amenábar and starring Nicole Kidman. Atmospheric and slow paced with a surprise ending.

Poltergeist (1982). Directed by Tobe Hooper. Starring Craig T. Nelson and JoBeth Williams. Produced and cowritten by Steven Spielberg. Ghosts, Spielberg style. Over the top with oodles of special effects. Scary entertainment at its best.

Sammy Terry Scary Tales (2003). Starring Bob Carter. Hosted by Sammy Terry. An anthology of true scary tales from Indiana, inspired by the book *Haunted Hoosier Trails* by folklorist Wanda Lou Willis.

Session 9 (2001). Directed by Brad Anderson. Starring David Caruso. An abandoned mental hospital reveals its secrets.

The Shining (1980). Directed by Stanley Kubrick and starring Jack Nicolson, Shelley Duvall, and Scatman Crothers. Stephen King's book had more ghostly influence than the movie, however the movie is the epitome of classic horror, combining a haunted hotel, a psychic child, and a writer gone mad.

Sightings: Heartland Ghost (2002). Directed by Brian Trenchard-Smith and starring Beau Bridges and Nia Long. Based on the true story of a haunted home and the television crew that attempted to film its paranormal activity.

The Sixth Sense (1999). Directed by M. Night Shyamalan. Starring Bruce Willis and Haley Joel Osment. Psychological suspense and a surprise ending.

Spooked: The Ghosts of Waverly Hills Sanatorium (2006). Directed by Christopher Saint Booth. A documentary filmed on location at Waverly Hills Sanatorium, a tuberculosis hospital near Louisville, Kentucky. More than sixty-five thousand people died at Waverly, and some call it the scariest place on earth.

Unsolved Mysteries: Ghosts (2004). Part of the *Unsolved Mysteries* series featuring famous ghost stories.

White Noise (2005). Directed by Geoffrey Sax. Starring Michael Keaton. A supernatural thriller that introduced electronic voice phenomenon to the masses.

APPENDIX D

Special Tours and Events

Crown Hill Cemetery. Voted the best walking tour in Indy by *Indianapolis Monthly* magazine, Crown Hill offers a wide variety of walking tours throughout the year. "Skeletons in the Closet" is a sunset tour featuring secrets and tragedies of some of Crown Hill's most notorious residents. Call (317) 920-2644. Web site: www.crownhill.org.

French Lick Resort and Casino. The Historic Landmarks Foundation offers a walking tour several times daily and on all holidays except Christmas Day. The seventy-minute guided tour narrates the fascinating history of the recently restored resort. Tours depart at 10:00 A.M., noon, 2:00 P.M., and 4:00 P.M. Purchase tickets at the circa 1901 Historic Landmarks Foundation shop located in the retail corridor north of the lobby. Call (812) 936-4034.

Hannah House. Year-round open house tours and special ghost tours in October. Also available for overnight stays particularly geared for ghost hunters. 3801 Madison Avenue, Indianapolis, IN 46227. Call (317) 787-8486. Web site: www.thehannahmansion.org.

Historic Indiana Ghost Walks and Tours. Year-round walking ghost tours through many historic areas in Indianapolis and surrounding areas. P.O. Box 687, Westfield, IN 46074. Call (317) 840-6456. Web site: www.unseenpress.com.

Historic Landmarks Foundation of Indiana. Offers walking and

186 GHOST HUNTER'S GUIDE TO INDIANAPOLIS

bus tours throughout the state of Indiana. The Hair-Raising History Tour is an annual motor coach tour of haunted historic sites in Indianapolis. The tour changes every year, but past sites include Tuckaway House and the Morris Butler home. Call (317) 639-4534, extension 143. Web site: www.historiclandmarks.org.

Indiana Medical History Museum. Located in the old pathology building on the grounds of the formal Central State Mental Hospital, the museum houses a collection of scientific artifacts from the beginning of scientific psychiatry and modern medicine in a completely authentic setting, including clinical laboratories, an amphitheater, and an autopsy room. Tours are available during operating hours. 3045 Vermont Street, Indianapolis, IN 46222. Call (317) 635-7329. Web site: www.imhm.org.

Irvington Halloween Festival. Since 1946, the historical neighborhood of Irvington has hosted a spirited event celebrating Halloween. Activities include classic monster movies, costume contests, food and craft booths, a parade, and a walking ghost tour. Usually held on the last weekend in October. Web site: www.halloweenfest.org.

Riley Days. One of the largest festivals in Indiana, celebrating the birthday of James Whitcomb Riley in Greenfield, Indiana. Usually held the first weekend in October, activities include pumpkin decorating, craft and food booths, and tours of Riley's boyhood home, which inspired many of his poems including *Little Orphant Annie.* 312 East Main Street, Suite C, Greenfield, IN. 46140. Call (317) 462-2141. Web site: www.rileyfestival.com.

Spirit Fest at Camp Chesterfield. Spirit Fest, a celebration of mind, body, and spirit, is an annual event at historic Camp Chesterfield. Enjoy psychic readers, psychic artists, free lectures, and body workers or stroll the landscaped grounds of this quaint and unusual village. Don't miss the Hett Art Gallery and Museum. Spirit Fest is usually held in September. Call (765) 378-0235. Web site: www.campchesterfield.net.

Whispers Estate Bed and Breakfast. Tours are available by appointment only. 714 West Warren Street, Mitchell, IN 47446. Call (812) 360-3718.

Wyandotte Caves. Nestled in the hills of Harrison-Crawford State Forest in southern Indiana, Wyandotte Caves have fascinated visitors for more than 150 years. The Monument Mountain Tour is available from May 1 to Labor Day weekend. The tour lasts approximately ninety minutes, and groups of twelve or more are eligible for a discount. 7315 Wyandotte Cave Road, Leavenworth, IN 47137. Call (888) 702-2837. Web site: www.wyandottecaves.com.

APPENDIX E

Organizations

American Institute of
Parapsychology
Thomasville, GA 31792
www.parapsychologylab.com

American Society for Psychical
Research
5 West Seventy-Third St.
New York, NY 10023
(212) 799-5050
www.aspr.com

Crossroads Paranormal
P. O. Box 5033
Lafayette, IN 47903
www.crossroadsparanormal.com

Ghost Research Society
P. O. Box 205
Oaklawn, IL 60454
(708) 425-5163
www.ghostresearch.org

Indiana Ghost Trackers
www.indianaghosts.org

Indiana Scientific Paranormal
Investigators
6021 Pennyworth Circle
Indianapolis, IN 46203
www.indianaspi.com

Indy Ghost Hunters
P. O. Box 39261
Indianapolis, IN 46239
www.indyghosthunters.com

International Ghost Hunters
Society
848 North Rainbow Blvd., #592
Las Vegas, NV 89107
www.ghostweb.com

International Society for
Paranormal Research
4712 Admiralty Way
Marina Del Ray, CA 90292
(323) 644-8866
www.ispr.net

New England Society for
Psychic Research

Mrs. Lorraine Warren
P. O. Box 41
Monroe, CT 06468
www.warrens.net

Parapsychology Foundation
Inc.
P. O. Box 1562
New York, NY 10021

(212) 628-1550
www.parapsychology.org

Rhine Research Center
Duke University
2741 Campus Walk Ave.
Durham, NC 27705
(919) 309-4600
www.rhine.org

APPENDIX F

Internet Resources

www.aaevp.com. American Association of Electronic Voice Phenomena, education resource on EVP including tips and techniques.

www.centerofpeace.com. Psychic Marilene Isaacs' Web site.

www.crossroadsparanormal.com. Web site for the Crossroads Paranormal ghost group. Includes events, news, and forums.

www.ghosthound.com. Site includes EVP, videos, photos, ghost stories, and online courses.

www.ghostmag.com. *Ghost!* magazine, an online and print magazine featuring national hauntings.

www.ghosts.org. Obiwan's UFO-Free Paranormal Page, one of the Internet's oldest ghost sites. Includes information, true ghost stories, photos, and links.

www.ghostvillage.com. Extensive site for paranormal information including news, directory, forums, library, and merchandise.

www.goldwave.com. Popular computer software for transferring and cleaning up EVP recordings.

www.hauntedhouses.com. Site includes great photos of haunted houses and descriptions of hauntings.

www.hauntedindiana.com. Web site for *Haunted Indiana* magazine.

www.hauntings.com. Web site for ISPR, the International Society for Paranormal Research, headed by Dr. Larry Montz.

www.indianaghosts.org. This is the main Web site for the statewide nonprofit ghost group the Indiana Ghost Trackers.

www.libraryghost.com. Live 24/7 ghost cam of the infamous Willard Library, reputed home of the ghostly Gray Lady, in Evansville, Indiana.

www.prairieghosts.com. Troy Taylor's comprehensive Web site with ghost stories, events, tour information, research, and bookstore.

www.rootsweb.com/~inpcrp. Indiana Pioneer Cemeteries Restoration Project. Site includes news, restoration-workshop dates, and legislation affecting Indiana cemeteries.

www.the-atlantic-paranormal-society.com. Web site for the TAPS ghost group and stars of the Sci Fi channel's *Ghost Hunters*.

www.thehannahmansion.org. Hannah House's official Web site includes information on the home's history, hauntings, tours, overnighters, and rental information for private functions.

www.theshadowlands.net/ghost. This Web site is one of the oldest and most comprehensive ghost sites, with Indiana hauntings extensively covered in its Haunted Places index.

Historical Societies and Museums

Brown County Historical Society
P. O. Box 668
Nashville, IN 47448
(812) 988-6089

Crawford County Historical
and Genealogical Society
P. O. Box 133
Leavenworth, IN 47137
e-mail: rockman@disknet.com

Hancock County Historical
Society
P. O. Box 375
Greenfield, IN 46140
(317) 462-7780

Hett Art Gallery and Museum
Camp Chesterfield
P. O. Box 132
Chesterfield, IN 46017
(765) 378-0235

Historic Landmarks Foundation
of Indiana
340 West Michigan St.

Indianapolis, IN 46202
(317) 639-4534

Hook's American Drug Store
Museum
Indiana State Fairgrounds
1180 East Thirty-Eighth St.
Indianapolis, IN 46205
(317) 951-2222

Indiana Historical Society
450 West Ohio St.
Indianapolis, IN 46202
(317) 232-1882
(800) 447-1830
www.indianahistory.org

Indiana Medical History Museum
Central State Mental Hospital
3045 Vermont St.
Indianapolis, IN 46222
(317) 635-7329
www.imhm.org

Indiana State Archives
6440 East Thirtieth St.

Indianapolis, IN 46219
(317) 591-5222

Irvington Historical Society
312 South Downey Ave.
Indianapolis, IN 46219
(317) 357-0318

James Whitcomb Riley
Birthplace and Museum
250 West Main St.
Greenfield, IN 46140
(317) 477-4340

James Whitcomb Riley Home
Museum
528 Lockerbie St.
Indianapolis, IN
(317) 631-5885

Lawrence County Historical
and Genealogical Society
929 Fifteenth St.
Bedford, IN 47421
(812) 278-8575

Madison County Historical
Society
15 West Eleventh St.
P. O. Box 696
Anderson, IN 46016

(765) 683-0052

Marion County Historical
Society
P. O. Box 2223
Indianapolis, IN 46206
e-mail: cahall726@aol.com

Orange County Historical
Society
P. O. Box 454
Paoli, IN 47454
e-mail: bak@kiva.net

President Benjamin Harrison
Home
1230 North Delaware St.
Indianapolis, IN 46202
(317) 631-1888

Tippecanoe Battlefield
Museum
200 Battle Ground Ave.
Battle Ground, IN 47920
(765) 476-8411

Tippecanoe County Historical
Association
1001 South St.
Lafayette, IN 47901
(765) 476-8411

BIBLIOGRAPHY

Drabek, Thomas. "Disaster in Aisle 13" *The Indianapolis Star*

Foor, Mel. "Claypool Well Known in Politics." *The Indianapolis Star* 7 Nov 1971:B9.

Indianapolis Monthly. 1989.

The Indianapolis Star.

Indiana State Archives.

Jones, Katina Z. *The Everything Palmistry Book: Discover What the Future Holds—Life, Love, and Wealth—All in the Palm of Your Hand.* Adam Media Corp, 2003.

Marimen, Mark. *Haunted Indiana 3.* Thunder Bay Press, 2003.

———. Haunted Indiana 4, Thunder Bay Press, 2005.

Miclot, Kay Joy. *Skiles Test and the House of Blue Lights.* Miclot, 1975.

Miner, Paul. *Indiana's Best! An Illustrated Celebration of the Indiana State Fairgrounds, 1852-1992."* Indianapolis: Prompt Publications, 1992.

Muncie, Larry. *Irvington Stories.* Invington Historical Society, 1992.

Nicolas, Anna. *The Story of Crown Hill.* Indianapolis: Crown Hill Association, 1928.

Thay, Edrick. *Ghost Stories of Indiana.* Lone Pine Publishing, 2002.

Tippecanoe County Historical Association.

Walton, Lloyd B. "History of Murat Temple."

Wyeth, John A. "Horrors of Camp Morton." *Century Magazine,* April 1891.

INDEX